This Cute Book Belongs To

____

____

Puzzle #1
SUMMER

LROFOPFOO   _ _ _ _ _ _ _ _ _

NEEERGVRE   _ _ _ _ _ _ _ _ _

NOIACNT   _ _ _ _ _ _ _

ALUNLYNA   _ _ _ _ _ _ _ _

CRDU   _ _ _ _

ZOLCA   _ _ _ _ _

UFEMERP   _ _ _ _ _ _ _

BNCAI   _ _ _ _ _

FDIEINNG   _ _ _ _ _ _ _ _

TOATS   _ _ _ _ _

IAINNKNM   _ _ _ _ _ _ _ _

SSEOOUS   _ _ _ _ _ _ _

MAGIC TRICKS

ANTATR   _ _ _ _ _ _

RGMOUWT   _ _ _ _ _ _ _

LOTCUC   _ _ _ _ _ _

REOOCJTRP   _ _ _ _ _ _ _ _ _

DERSUC   _ _ _ _ _ _

RRCNJUOO   _ _ _ _ _ _ _ _

IHLBDRUN   _ _ _ _ _ _ _ _

OJEUNCR   _ _ _ _ _ _ _

ROUNCYJ   _ _ _ _ _ _ _

EXIPI   _ _ _ _ _

DAMZEA   _ _ _ _ _ _

RCAHM   _ _ _ _ _

IOSCNOTTAR

_ _ _ _ _ _ _ _ _ _

MCLFIOMIR

_ _ _ _ _ _ _ _ _

HCRALSO

_ _ _ _ _ _ _

ASGET

_ _ _ _ _

RIANRBILA

_ _ _ _ _ _ _ _ _

EEEOKPBOKR

_ _ _ _ _ _ _ _ _ _

KSMDAA

_ _ _ _ _ _

PROM

_ _ _ _

NUDRO

_ _ _ _ _

PCONSIROMA

_ _ _ _ _ _ _ _ _ _

RPTTAE

_ _ _ _ _ _

TBLIEGR

_ _ _ _ _ _ _

FUNNY

YHIRATLI

_ _ _ _ _ _ _ _

QPUI

_ _ _ _

AEOPTNTYLIL

_ _ _ _ _ _ _ _ _ _ _

IWYMSH

_ _ _ _ _ _

LFACIRCA

_ _ _ _ _ _ _ _

EITTAUTNONA

_ _ _ _ _ _ _ _ _ _ _

HSCU

_ _ _ _

YPROAD

_ _ _ _ _ _

ABDARTS

_ _ _ _ _ _ _

IMCNYAD

_ _ _ _ _ _ _

NICCEKH

_ _ _ _ _ _ _

SFCEE

_ _ _ _ _

Puzzle #5
MODEL TRAINS

DREVI   _ _ _ _ _

CCREROT   _ _ _ _ _ _ _

TMOAHPN   _ _ _ _ _ _ _

SPHEOWEP   _ _ _ _ _ _ _ _

MRNHAOSE   _ _ _ _ _ _ _ _

LACSE   _ _ _ _ _

UACCARCY   _ _ _ _ _ _ _ _

TNEROM   _ _ _ _ _ _

TTUPICAYLNU   _ _ _ _ _ _ _ _ _ _ _

EGRFROE   _ _ _ _ _ _ _

RAYLTEAHCP   _ _ _ _ _ _ _ _ _ _

OYRMFITCNO   _ _ _ _ _ _ _ _ _ _

MAIL

ERABTE

_ _ _ _ _ _

YAST

_ _ _ _

DUAFR

_ _ _ _ _ _

TNEIND

_ _ _ _ _ _

EGSA

_ _ _ _

ODNDLLAR

_ _ _ _ _ _ _ _

ERRVSE

_ _ _ _ _ _

AFROG

_ _ _ _ _

EGTLUANT

_ _ _ _ _ _ _ _

CTAATSROINN

_ _ _ _ _ _ _ _ _ _ _

ERIALT

_ _ _ _ _ _

PSOT

_ _ _ _

ART

ETIMRS _ _ _ _ _ _

EATNRIUIM _ _ _ _ _ _ _ _ _

RIMIVTIPE _ _ _ _ _ _ _ _ _

NAFYC _ _ _ _ _

HATICRLAET _ _ _ _ _ _ _ _ _ _

ETEAHRT _ _ _ _ _ _ _

TURVSOOI _ _ _ _ _ _ _ _

ARENYNT _ _ _ _ _ _ _

PLTETAE _ _ _ _ _ _ _

MOIID _ _ _ _ _

CPRACETI _ _ _ _ _ _ _ _

UPSO _ _ _ _

Puzzle #8
MONEY

LLASM   _ _ _ _ _

LIOUDIQANTI   _ _ _ _ _ _ _ _ _ _ _

TOLO   _ _ _ _

UUYRS   _ _ _ _ _

KOOH   _ _ _ _

EKIT   _ _ _ _

RTAEBR   _ _ _ _ _ _

TSNMISA   _ _ _ _ _ _ _

VSNGAI   _ _ _ _ _ _

HCEESE   _ _ _ _ _ _

LRNDEE   _ _ _ _ _ _

UOSTMC   _ _ _ _ _ _

STAMP COLLECTING

PITNMRI   _ _ _ _ _ _ _

HEAURSRGC   _ _ _ _ _ _ _ _ _

REDNESCNO   _ _ _ _ _ _ _ _ _

VARGE   _ _ _ _ _

OCLAIONTL   _ _ _ _ _ _ _ _ _

NTLIPGA   _ _ _ _ _ _ _

TNHYOLAOG   _ _ _ _ _ _ _ _ _

ORIOTC   _ _ _ _ _ _

PRNOEUD   _ _ _ _ _ _ _

LMLI   _ _ _ _

LIEHIILBBPO   _ _ _ _ _ _ _ _ _ _ _

VREMESPIIS   _ _ _ _ _ _ _ _ _ _

Puzzle #10
FASHION

HOKO   _ _ _ _

HCLEE   _ _ _ _ _

MILYTE   _ _ _ _ _ _

RSTELPSETER   _ _ _ _ _ _ _ _ _ _

EEROPTTL   _ _ _ _ _ _ _ _

NDGILOME   _ _ _ _ _ _ _ _

MLUBEM   _ _ _ _ _ _

TTTIRABUE   _ _ _ _ _ _ _ _ _

RFMNIO   _ _ _ _ _ _

GSDSEOD   _ _ _ _ _ _ _

ALMBRCSE   _ _ _ _ _ _ _ _

EAKTS   _ _ _ _ _

BOUNDARIES

TMMENNOU _ _ _ _ _ _ _ _

RLAI _ _ _ _

TPIRCENC _ _ _ _ _ _ _ _

YARLIIL _ _ _ _ _ _ _

EIANFEDBL _ _ _ _ _ _ _ _ _

VIOIONTAL _ _ _ _ _ _ _ _ _

OANTICID _ _ _ _ _ _ _ _

NMELAIFT _ _ _ _ _ _ _ _

ECPRNISOSO _ _ _ _ _ _ _ _ _ _

BONUD _ _ _ _ _

CODIFNUNEN _ _ _ _ _ _ _ _ _ _

RVSEYU _ _ _ _ _ _

Puzzle #12
ORIGINAL

EANR

_ _ _ _

RPSTI

_ _ _ _ _

IANCTT

_ _ _ _ _ _

ENEIMPERTX

_ _ _ _ _ _ _ _ _ _

TRRUCOP

_ _ _ _ _ _ _

OERAMETSL

_ _ _ _ _ _ _ _ _

YCIADNM

_ _ _ _ _ _ _

OGWR

_ _ _ _

RDFOEM

_ _ _ _ _ _

TRKSDICAE

_ _ _ _ _ _ _ _ _

TITWS

_ _ _ _ _

ERTEVPDER

_ _ _ _ _ _ _ _ _

Puzzle #13
WOMEN EMPOWERMENT

ANSOPRO   _ _ _ _ _ _ _

DERSUT   _ _ _ _ _ _

OSYNIOSMGU   _ _ _ _ _ _ _ _ _ _

MLCTICCAREI   _ _ _ _ _ _ _ _ _ _ _

SEXISM   _ _ _ _ _ _

AUKBR   _ _ _ _ _

LFOW   _ _ _ _

YNSIMOIGSM   _ _ _ _ _ _ _ _ _ _

OAPCBM   _ _ _ _ _ _

RSEREIBAS   _ _ _ _ _ _ _ _ _

MSIMIFNE   _ _ _ _ _ _ _ _

PEMRUTC   _ _ _ _ _ _ _

TIME MANAGEMENT

STAIENCN
_ _ _ _ _ _ _ _

ASSEPAG
_ _ _ _ _ _ _

ESBOILEPNRS
_ _ _ _ _ _ _ _ _ _ _

TSMOHRE
_ _ _ _ _ _ _

NNGINUR
_ _ _ _ _ _ _

ICUAGOSSA
_ _ _ _ _ _ _ _ _

IJFYF
_ _ _ _ _

TTNAARCS
_ _ _ _ _ _ _ _

FIYRLBE
_ _ _ _ _ _ _

EUTTPR
_ _ _ _ _ _

ESGPAPOT
_ _ _ _ _ _ _ _

TLTLEI
_ _ _ _ _ _

Puzzle #15
PERSONAL FINANCE

HCOTU   _ _ _ _ _

SPEAATER   _ _ _ _ _ _ _ _

VUREEEN   _ _ _ _ _ _ _

WATN   _ _ _ _

IARSAMCH   _ _ _ _ _ _ _ _

RBELLIA   _ _ _ _ _ _ _

REARIFM   _ _ _ _ _ _ _

AGMTZEIEN   _ _ _ _ _ _ _ _ _

EITRLECD   _ _ _ _ _ _ _ _

AIFSONH   _ _ _ _ _ _ _

TIBERM   _ _ _ _ _ _

RCEONR   _ _ _ _ _ _

Puzzle #16
GARDEN

OBMCXOC   _ _ _ _ _ _ _

TSKOC   _ _ _ _ _

CREA   _ _ _ _

EGSLOASUSH   _ _ _ _ _ _ _ _ _ _

EEBNTN   _ _ _ _ _ _

EREARTC   _ _ _ _ _ _ _

PAGDOA   _ _ _ _ _ _

PNOE   _ _ _ _

RLYEGLA   _ _ _ _ _ _ _

RYRCKOE   _ _ _ _ _ _ _

BDNRA   _ _ _ _ _

TSPE   _ _ _ _

LORATTUININ   _ _ _ _ _ _ _ _ _ _ _

URNSE   _ _ _ _ _

ERTHEROOPHT   _ _ _ _ _ _ _ _ _ _ _

JEEJNU   _ _ _ _ _ _

CONNTIFU   _ _ _ _ _ _ _ _

PANS   _ _ _ _

OTAAIIXTNND   _ _ _ _ _ _ _ _ _ _ _

IALYROOGGBO   _ _ _ _ _ _ _ _ _ _ _

SIHTARIC   _ _ _ _ _ _ _ _

ETEIDICT   _ _ _ _ _ _ _ _

CUFENI   _ _ _ _ _ _

ORIOSSHCL   _ _ _ _ _ _ _ _ _

BASKETBALL

BREUNDO

_ _ _ _ _ _ _

GITVIOMATN

_ _ _ _ _ _ _ _ _ _

VALTREYIITS

_ _ _ _ _ _ _ _ _ _ _

OPST

_ _ _ _

DOHAWDRO

_ _ _ _ _ _ _ _

ICNIVOTNAO

_ _ _ _ _ _ _ _ _ _

ETLGA

_ _ _ _ _

EDFT

_ _ _ _

MIITGNDNAO

_ _ _ _ _ _ _ _ _ _

LCOANTIOSNO

_ _ _ _ _ _ _ _ _ _ _

YTIINIBAL

_ _ _ _ _ _ _ _ _

RCTNOEV

_ _ _ _ _ _ _

CHINA

OOBACTC

_ _ _ _ _ _ _

IAEELGW

_ _ _ _ _ _ _

OMSRMASCI

_ _ _ _ _ _ _ _ _

NSAI

_ _ _ _

HNLOAWC

_ _ _ _ _ _ _

ONGKME

_ _ _ _ _ _

KWANNTUGG

_ _ _ _ _ _ _ _ _

EBIHE

_ _ _ _ _

ULPIC

_ _ _ _ _

DLALRO

_ _ _ _ _ _

OXERB

_ _ _ _ _

BCSAAU

_ _ _ _ _ _

GAME

WTTIERS   _ _ _ _ _ _ _

OTIPN   _ _ _ _ _

LEDA   _ _ _ _

YKPO   _ _ _ _

CILK   _ _ _ _

VRKEEO   _ _ _ _ _ _

WRENIN   _ _ _ _ _ _

OOAHW   _ _ _ _ _

EBDIGR   _ _ _ _ _ _

SKEAT   _ _ _ _ _

IZQU   _ _ _ _

MCAP   _ _ _ _

ABOONB   _ _ _ _ _ _

INPRAMISO   _ _ _ _ _ _ _ _ _

YNGEMBAA   _ _ _ _ _ _ _ _

UMKS   _ _ _ _

TEERPYRSB   _ _ _ _ _ _ _ _ _

ESRECS   _ _ _ _ _ _

ERLAY   _ _ _ _ _

AYRAMNAA   _ _ _ _ _ _ _ _

SBRSA   _ _ _ _ _

OURCIUS   _ _ _ _ _ _ _

OUSIPELR   _ _ _ _ _ _ _ _

TNEUPA   _ _ _ _ _ _

RITESEL

_ _ _ _ _ _ _

LEUSNITACR

_ _ _ _ _ _ _ _ _ _

WGLLNDIE

_ _ _ _ _ _ _ _

MTLTOEA

_ _ _ _ _ _ _

FWERELA

_ _ _ _ _ _ _

ICHTP

_ _ _ _ _

AGHROPNEA

_ _ _ _ _ _ _ _ _

TOTNCINSSE

_ _ _ _ _ _ _ _ _ _

STUADETI

_ _ _ _ _ _ _ _

OHSEU

_ _ _ _ _

CHZEC

_ _ _ _ _

AHNIAAGN

_ _ _ _ _ _ _ _

Puzzle #23
HOTEL

ARNIINTTE

_ _ _ _ _ _ _ _ _

EEPK

_ _ _ _

AAGROENPT

_ _ _ _ _ _ _ _ _

AEFC

_ _ _ _

MOAND

_ _ _ _ _

POLEEERHTKE

_ _ _ _ _ _ _ _ _ _ _

DRERI

_ _ _ _ _

BEHPLOL

_ _ _ _ _ _ _

ORTEPR

_ _ _ _ _ _

SYPGESAWAA

_ _ _ _ _ _ _ _ _ _

RGDNA

_ _ _ _ _

SANERGSAME

_ _ _ _ _ _ _ _ _ _

UNERNR   _ _ _ _ _ _

BTALOL   _ _ _ _ _ _

EIENFAC   _ _ _ _ _ _ _

OMNRSIMEI   _ _ _ _ _ _ _ _ _

ACYL   _ _ _ _

GEETRAWAA   _ _ _ _ _ _ _ _ _

RWEAVEON   _ _ _ _ _ _ _ _

NLGALAI   _ _ _ _ _ _ _

HATCW   _ _ _ _ _

ALTME   _ _ _ _ _

TDEMTA   _ _ _ _ _ _

INPYDLO   _ _ _ _ _ _ _

STRING ART

ANNLTUGE

_ _ _ _ _ _ _ _

OEYTHR

_ _ _ _ _ _

EFTR

_ _ _ _

TETLAR

_ _ _ _ _ _

RACTECAUIR

_ _ _ _ _ _ _ _ _ _

CRIDROP

_ _ _ _ _ _ _

ITAVOANI

_ _ _ _ _ _ _ _

AGSCSYNTMI

_ _ _ _ _ _ _ _ _ _

MILEUSASRR

_ _ _ _ _ _ _ _ _ _

NIEL

_ _ _ _

LEKI

_ _ _ _

LIEDRSLITY

_ _ _ _ _ _ _ _ _ _

Puzzle #26
TABLE TENNIS

AOCNN   _ _ _ _ _

IEINTS   _ _ _ _ _ _

TWROH   _ _ _ _ _

CASLCSI   _ _ _ _ _ _ _

GEELDN   _ _ _ _ _ _

PFLA   _ _ _ _

EAYRPL   _ _ _ _ _ _

AIARN   _ _ _ _ _

YROHNOCGOL _ _ _ _ _ _ _ _ _ _

SHAUSQ   _ _ _ _ _ _

YISTX   _ _ _ _ _

YHERCR   _ _ _ _ _ _

Puzzle #27

GERMAN SHEPHERD

ORMST   _ _ _ _ _

DGIAD   _ _ _ _ _

TLOLRE   _ _ _ _ _ _

UCRELNE   _ _ _ _ _ _ _

NEILAADHN _ _ _ _ _ _ _ _ _

KEZKNEUHAR _ _ _ _ _ _ _ _ _ _

EHRHSSEDPES _ _ _ _ _ _ _ _ _ _ _

EUNADB   _ _ _ _ _ _

ERANNGNEBT _ _ _ _ _ _ _ _ _ _

RHDEER   _ _ _ _ _ _

TAORSP   _ _ _ _ _ _

REPDEHSH   _ _ _ _ _ _ _ _

FRUIT

GEEDRA   _ _ _ _ _ _

EPSEYL   _ _ _ _ _ _

TOOTAM   _ _ _ _ _ _

EIMLY   _ _ _ _ _

MEAFEL   _ _ _ _ _ _

ALBBMRE   _ _ _ _ _ _ _

UHIORSS   _ _ _ _ _ _ _

EYRRETAB   _ _ _ _ _ _ _ _

TOMIFC   _ _ _ _ _ _ _

HLOETACTR   _ _ _ _ _ _ _ _ _

IINORUTF   _ _ _ _ _ _ _ _

AANILVL   _ _ _ _ _ _ _

TEUBEMOANN   _ _ _ _ _ _ _ _ _ _

EALD   _ _ _ _

ATOCBTINII   _ _ _ _ _ _ _ _ _ _

SOTLLEFAR   _ _ _ _ _ _ _ _ _

CAVROEUSDA   _ _ _ _ _ _ _ _ _ _

STRUC   _ _ _ _ _

UBNLT   _ _ _ _ _

NEIRP   _ _ _ _ _

ALICV   _ _ _ _ _

JKILLYO   _ _ _ _ _ _ _

EOSNEIDPRN   _ _ _ _ _ _ _ _ _ _

UBREMALL   _ _ _ _ _ _ _ _

PUZZLE

ICAHGLNEGNL   _ _ _ _ _ _ _ _ _ _ _

EOPRHT   _ _ _ _ _ _

YCAHTC   _ _ _ _ _ _

ZUQI   _ _ _ _

ESLBACRB   _ _ _ _ _ _ _ _

TAENLGNE   _ _ _ _ _ _ _ _

OMDFBUDUN   _ _ _ _ _ _ _ _ _

CNTNOCE   _ _ _ _ _ _ _

NAEEBT   _ _ _ _ _ _

CITSK   _ _ _ _ _

UERQE   _ _ _ _ _

WREDNNTOME   _ _ _ _ _ _ _ _ _ _

COPNYA

_ _ _ _ _ _

IOCTLOP

_ _ _ _ _ _ _

UCPAATLT

_ _ _ _ _ _ _ _

NEEUPDSRGDO

_ _ _ _ _ _ _ _ _ _ _

ONPAR

_ _ _ _ _

MNITEUTRNS

_ _ _ _ _ _ _ _ _ _

NACDRA

_ _ _ _ _ _

UFEL

_ _ _ _

BRAADO

_ _ _ _ _ _

EHLD

_ _ _ _

YARAIW

_ _ _ _ _ _

UOCTNWOHD

_ _ _ _ _ _ _ _ _

WORKING

OREUTR _ _ _ _ _ _

LSWAOLW _ _ _ _ _ _ _

THNGLIGI _ _ _ _ _ _ _ _

TUOVENLIO _ _ _ _ _ _ _ _ _

NIUAFPL _ _ _ _ _ _ _

RNYYGES _ _ _ _ _ _ _

LTSPI _ _ _ _ _

PTREAIV _ _ _ _ _ _ _

CRSTEE _ _ _ _ _ _

GRNENIGINEE _ _ _ _ _ _ _ _ _ _ _

OHVRITSEG _ _ _ _ _ _ _ _ _

NKAB _ _ _ _

Puzzle #33
POTATO

MRUHPY   _ _ _ _ _ _

NOMLUSA   _ _ _ _ _ _ _

COTQETREU   _ _ _ _ _ _ _ _ _

OGSCRNSE   _ _ _ _ _ _ _ _

TOAR   _ _ _ _

NEILNMA   _ _ _ _ _ _ _

UBRTE   _ _ _ _ _

TTTYA   _ _ _ _ _

LFTALHUEH   _ _ _ _ _ _ _ _ _

EARHCUHA   _ _ _ _ _ _ _ _

NSIEDI   _ _ _ _ _ _

LIPE   _ _ _ _

RYRSAT

_ _ _ _ _ _

MGAI

_ _ _ _

TLASTRE

_ _ _ _ _ _ _

DWRAF

_ _ _ _ _

DOURCEVAAS

_ _ _ _ _ _ _ _ _ _

AFRESLOTRW

_ _ _ _ _ _ _ _ _ _

ILURSNAG

_ _ _ _ _ _ _ _

TGYLEOVIN

_ _ _ _ _ _ _ _ _

HAORNPAA

_ _ _ _ _ _ _ _

EOMBIROLA

_ _ _ _ _ _ _ _ _

MRYELE

_ _ _ _ _ _

IEETGRSP

_ _ _ _ _ _ _ _

Puzzle #35
SUPER CAR

EOECRDNSN   _ _ _ _ _ _ _ _ _

MERDMI   _ _ _ _ _ _

NGAF   _ _ _ _

MRCUB   _ _ _ _ _

IRGUNNN   _ _ _ _ _ _ _

RHSOACER   _ _ _ _ _ _ _ _

OCRADAL   _ _ _ _ _ _ _

KPRA   _ _ _ _

RLEDNEI   _ _ _ _ _ _ _

TAACR   _ _ _ _ _

IEOTMV   _ _ _ _ _ _

INMEAHC   _ _ _ _ _ _ _

Puzzle #36
BICYCLE

ORTSCKEP   _ _ _ _ _ _ _ _

ETGASRGEE   _ _ _ _ _ _ _ _ _

TBUE   _ _ _ _

ACEL   _ _ _ _

HRETSFI   _ _ _ _ _ _ _

NSCGIHCOR   _ _ _ _ _ _ _ _ _

PYCIESF   _ _ _ _ _ _ _

YCELEXREC   _ _ _ _ _ _ _ _ _

CBAEDRI   _ _ _ _ _ _ _

PMDEO   _ _ _ _ _

BTMOOIRKE   _ _ _ _ _ _ _ _ _

IRMLOTEMEE   _ _ _ _ _ _ _ _ _ _

KNITTING

GLEAYR

_ _ _ _ _ _

OMSMYISPU

_ _ _ _ _ _ _ _ _

CERDAESE

_ _ _ _ _ _ _ _

ETUSRU

_ _ _ _ _ _

ETRTPUM

_ _ _ _ _ _ _

ARICBF

_ _ _ _ _ _

EELNDE

_ _ _ _ _ _

REIONM

_ _ _ _ _ _

MHRAISFNE

_ _ _ _ _ _ _ _ _

STTCIH

_ _ _ _ _ _

CIOTRT

_ _ _ _ _ _

EXTTLEI

_ _ _ _ _ _ _

PEOPLE

SCOENH

_ _ _ _ _ _

RMRUUO

_ _ _ _ _ _

ATEHR

_ _ _ _ _

ECNOREF

_ _ _ _ _ _ _

YTCONU

_ _ _ _ _ _

DEAG

_ _ _ _

RAWNNDA

_ _ _ _ _ _ _

ENORARWIPB

_ _ _ _ _ _ _ _ _ _

ACUUIDOSA

_ _ _ _ _ _ _ _ _

ENMYE

_ _ _ _ _

KONNW

_ _ _ _ _

ADNGR

_ _ _ _ _

LEFERI

_ _ _ _ _ _

RTCOASAEL

_ _ _ _ _ _ _ _ _

LIGLSIAOCT

_ _ _ _ _ _ _ _ _ _

MUDMY

_ _ _ _ _

EREGESTGA

_ _ _ _ _ _ _ _ _

ECRINALG

_ _ _ _ _ _ _ _

EOSFTTML

_ _ _ _ _ _ _ _

OTDOPAF

_ _ _ _ _ _ _

PLCOEUT

_ _ _ _ _ _ _

BAKC

_ _ _ _

NHTE

_ _ _ _

ALRNS

_ _ _ _ _

ELTGLU   _ _ _ _ _ _

NSGUUF   _ _ _ _ _ _

TEIAHBWIT   _ _ _ _ _ _ _ _ _

EREDES   _ _ _ _ _ _

SIOL   _ _ _ _

PEHADHSSEE   _ _ _ _ _ _ _ _ _ _

FINRMAG   _ _ _ _ _ _ _

WRLRGOE   _ _ _ _ _ _ _

UOHGR   _ _ _ _ _

CBOIA   _ _ _ _ _

ENIADARM   _ _ _ _ _ _ _ _

CHEK   _ _ _ _

LUPTIP   _ _ _ _ _ _

FMAR   _ _ _ _

CGANHE   _ _ _ _ _ _

NDECINTI   _ _ _ _ _ _ _ _

EFER   _ _ _ _

OBOEARNLH   _ _ _ _ _ _ _ _ _

LPEAAC   _ _ _ _ _ _

RSBIEC   _ _ _ _ _ _

VAWLAO   _ _ _ _ _ _

RCAIELT   _ _ _ _ _ _ _

RAENEDIVLEC   _ _ _ _ _ _ _ _ _ _ _

IRIUTMRV   _ _ _ _ _ _ _ _

Puzzle #42
HOME

TAYS   _ _ _ _

ISON   _ _ _ _

LBHUME   _ _ _ _ _ _

HNOE   _ _ _ _

SSREOD   _ _ _ _ _ _

UMCEOMT   _ _ _ _ _ _ _

NUTR   _ _ _ _

FHEOMOKL   _ _ _ _ _ _ _ _

ECERHSC   _ _ _ _ _ _ _

IOGWERLNEKT   _ _ _ _ _ _ _ _ _ _ _

EHLOW   _ _ _ _ _

PTYAR   _ _ _ _ _

IMPORTANCE OF WATER

LIACYLTIRC _ _ _ _ _ _ _ _ _ _

LTYUMIHI _ _ _ _ _ _ _ _

TMEEPL _ _ _ _ _ _

LRKOEVOO _ _ _ _ _ _ _ _

UESBACTSN _ _ _ _ _ _ _ _ _

HERE _ _ _ _

NAVITLAEUDO _ _ _ _ _ _ _ _ _ _ _

ALNTREC _ _ _ _ _ _ _

IRILPCAPN _ _ _ _ _ _ _ _ _

RTEGSENSA _ _ _ _ _ _ _ _ _

EBTA _ _ _ _

SAOWEHMT _ _ _ _ _ _ _ _

WIND SURFING

NKBCIGA   _ _ _ _ _ _ _

MIRMRET   _ _ _ _ _ _ _

ARPVO   _ _ _ _ _

SFUIRUO   _ _ _ _ _ _ _

NGHSETTR   _ _ _ _ _ _ _ _

IKKC   _ _ _ _

AWER   _ _ _ _

IDNW   _ _ _ _

TEAS   _ _ _ _

OLUF   _ _ _ _

SLTIOBAA   _ _ _ _ _ _ _ _

LCUR   _ _ _ _

Puzzle #45
SOLAR ENERGY

RVEVE

_ _ _ _ _

RAITVAL

_ _ _ _ _ _ _

RREENEGTEA

_ _ _ _ _ _ _ _ _ _

AULEROE

_ _ _ _ _ _ _

EIBLAETTDI

_ _ _ _ _ _ _ _ _ _

OHWUREPOES

_ _ _ _ _ _ _ _ _ _

ETIR

_ _ _ _

HLAB

_ _ _ _

ARPIRE

_ _ _ _ _ _

NQUKECI

_ _ _ _ _ _ _

NDPSE

_ _ _ _ _

LOWRE

_ _ _ _ _

Puzzle #46

MOVIE

EFOGNRI   _ _ _ _ _ _ _

TISCMSA   _ _ _ _ _ _ _

TAIEEMN   _ _ _ _ _ _ _

DCCIEENNY   _ _ _ _ _ _ _ _ _

NUHNAMTAL   _ _ _ _ _ _ _ _ _

IERDIOTNN   _ _ _ _ _ _ _ _ _

LOGEBTO   _ _ _ _ _ _ _

DTATICINO   _ _ _ _ _ _ _ _ _

GPLU   _ _ _ _

EPSYK   _ _ _ _ _

IPERATMESCE   _ _ _ _ _ _ _ _ _ _ _

HWINUDOT   _ _ _ _ _ _ _ _

Puzzle #47
TOMATO

FTIRU

_ _ _ _ _

UCGOMELAA

_ _ _ _ _ _ _ _ _

ESKUCR

_ _ _ _ _ _

DNRIREG

_ _ _ _ _ _ _

TSEPA

_ _ _ _ _

CMHEAELB

_ _ _ _ _ _ _ _

IDREANLME

_ _ _ _ _ _ _ _ _

OYRG

_ _ _ _

ISNPXH

_ _ _ _ _ _

LYIHPSAS

_ _ _ _ _ _ _ _

IYSPC

_ _ _ _ _

ALOITTLOM

_ _ _ _ _ _ _ _ _

OCRNAH

_ _ _ _ _ _

BEAS

_ _ _ _

ELATSHSIB

_ _ _ _ _ _ _ _ _

NITSEWS

_ _ _ _ _ _ _

ANVICTAXEO

_ _ _ _ _ _ _ _ _ _

STLOO

_ _ _ _ _

OGLN

_ _ _ _

NISEW

_ _ _ _ _

OTRO

_ _ _ _

ETPIMEES

_ _ _ _ _ _ _ _

NLSIGE

_ _ _ _ _ _

MMRTAINFE

_ _ _ _ _ _ _ _ _

Puzzle #49
SHOPPING

PLWSRA   _ _ _ _ _ _

ORAHNC   _ _ _ _ _ _

AZALP   _ _ _ _ _

TADER   _ _ _ _ _

WTON   _ _ _ _

RYARH   _ _ _ _ _

FLOOALTF   _ _ _ _ _ _ _ _

YDDOW   _ _ _ _ _

OEPMEYEL   _ _ _ _ _ _ _ _

PEITCDAN   _ _ _ _ _ _ _ _

AMDI   _ _ _ _

TNENOSC   _ _ _ _ _ _ _

ULINPK

_ _ _ _ _ _

DROON

_ _ _ _ _

ECNET

_ _ _ _ _

NSYC

_ _ _ _

NSCUIHO

_ _ _ _ _ _ _

TNGAREIMS

_ _ _ _ _ _ _ _ _

DDAOIRN

_ _ _ _ _ _ _

PPUIYE

_ _ _ _ _ _

CELAAT

_ _ _ _ _ _

TAWH

_ _ _ _

PNLAT

_ _ _ _ _

CUSD

_ _ _ _

Puzzle #51
STUDENT

RMFORE

_ _ _ _ _ _

SNULITTAAR

_ _ _ _ _ _ _ _ _ _

PICPAETRETI

_ _ _ _ _ _ _ _ _ _ _

IATMSNRO

_ _ _ _ _ _ _ _

OAUDSISUS

_ _ _ _ _ _ _ _ _

LSCAAIBT

_ _ _ _ _ _ _ _

EDNTTUS

_ _ _ _ _ _ _

RUTTO

_ _ _ _ _

STHFIELSS

_ _ _ _ _ _ _ _ _

OATIDIGNNIN

_ _ _ _ _ _ _ _ _ _ _

YATRTRFENI

_ _ _ _ _ _ _ _ _ _

RPHMOOGNA

_ _ _ _ _ _ _ _ _

DESCRIBE YOURSELF

TOCNEUR _ _ _ _ _ _ _

TOTSINA _ _ _ _ _ _ _

IFDITENY _ _ _ _ _ _ _ _

EEATRGAGXE _ _ _ _ _ _ _ _ _ _

ESESN _ _ _ _ _

ZINEDMOE _ _ _ _ _ _ _ _

ESUEEZQ _ _ _ _ _ _ _

EDIPR _ _ _ _ _

ERSNCE _ _ _ _ _ _

RSAANSCEU _ _ _ _ _ _ _ _ _

UOETLQEN _ _ _ _ _ _ _ _

HCEESP _ _ _ _ _ _

OFFICE

RLUE

_ _ _ _

OLRAYAM

_ _ _ _ _ _ _

LSTEEAGHIP

_ _ _ _ _ _ _ _ _ _

FLLI

_ _ _ _

HPEIASHD

_ _ _ _ _ _ _ _

OGLOM

_ _ _ _ _

RATTMOSESP

_ _ _ _ _ _ _ _ _ _

ERHI

_ _ _ _

RMETTERNEI

_ _ _ _ _ _ _ _ _ _

ATYCRRIAPH

_ _ _ _ _ _ _ _ _ _

VODI

_ _ _ _

CAENDMHTET

_ _ _ _ _ _ _ _ _ _

CYBER CRIME

LEFON

_ _ _ _ _

SAUEB

_ _ _ _ _

TEMNANCNEEH

_ _ _ _ _ _ _ _ _ _ _

SCIK

_ _ _ _

ADIR

_ _ _ _

CURNAEYTB

_ _ _ _ _ _ _ _ _

SIYDEACNT

_ _ _ _ _ _ _ _ _

UBRLRGA

_ _ _ _ _ _ _

ANGG

_ _ _ _

NESVGTIETIA

_ _ _ _ _ _ _ _ _ _ _

LAUDICIS

_ _ _ _ _ _ _ _

WETAGAY

_ _ _ _ _ _ _

Puzzle #55
TELEVISION

EECEM

_ _ _ _ _

OTAFGEO

_ _ _ _ _ _ _

NDEYCOAUMRT

_ _ _ _ _ _ _ _ _ _ _

CYULBTIPI

_ _ _ _ _ _ _ _ _

IERLLF

_ _ _ _ _ _

SECASC

_ _ _ _ _ _

GFERFA

_ _ _ _ _ _

RTCESHT

_ _ _ _ _ _ _

DPEURCRO

_ _ _ _ _ _ _ _

RFOAMT

_ _ _ _ _ _

ENIL

_ _ _ _

URAAPETCSCL

_ _ _ _ _ _ _ _ _ _ _

BUILDING

OBHRATMO

_ _ _ _ _ _ _ _

ILFNOOGR

_ _ _ _ _ _ _ _

IURMUMBNA

_ _ _ _ _ _ _ _ _

VAORLY

_ _ _ _ _ _

RIUN

_ _ _ _

EWPES

_ _ _ _ _

ORALMKCOO

_ _ _ _ _ _ _ _ _

RSICCU

_ _ _ _ _ _

SACAANDR

_ _ _ _ _ _ _ _

IEERGHMAT

_ _ _ _ _ _ _ _ _

ERGIGYP

_ _ _ _ _ _ _

ERLSBIT

_ _ _ _ _ _ _

MAKING WINE

INRDK   _ _ _ _ _

TLCIIENDBA   _ _ _ _ _ _ _ _ _ _

DBOY   _ _ _ _

LRAAMSA   _ _ _ _ _ _ _

SRLPGNKAI   _ _ _ _ _ _ _ _ _

GNZAIAM   _ _ _ _ _ _ _

TIPON   _ _ _ _ _

RIOL   _ _ _ _

LNNGAEPIL   _ _ _ _ _ _ _ _ _

GIRDEGOS   _ _ _ _ _ _ _ _

YMYGUZR   _ _ _ _ _ _ _

ILSYK   _ _ _ _ _

LITERATURE

ENSIUNRAT   _ _ _ _ _ _ _ _ _

VDAE   _ _ _ _

HEETM   _ _ _ _ _

XIEND   _ _ _ _ _

LOOIPGYLH   _ _ _ _ _ _ _ _ _

REDEAR   _ _ _ _ _ _

ICEQRTIU   _ _ _ _ _ _ _ _

DRUE   _ _ _ _

OAITQTOUN   _ _ _ _ _ _ _ _ _

NRSASAPSU   _ _ _ _ _ _ _ _ _

TISRRAUESL   _ _ _ _ _ _ _ _ _ _

ARRDE   _ _ _ _ _

Puzzle #59
GIRL EDUCATION

TPOTEACTI   _ _ _ _ _ _ _ _ _

LWHPE   _ _ _ _ _

IYBDD   _ _ _ _ _

SDNIEIHF   _ _ _ _ _ _ _ _

ERIP   _ _ _ _

PLHSY   _ _ _ _ _

EVLUA   _ _ _ _ _

CSHOLO   _ _ _ _ _ _

RCTEOJP   _ _ _ _ _ _ _

EDEVIPDR   _ _ _ _ _ _ _ _

CEEATDDU   _ _ _ _ _ _ _ _

PMIR   _ _ _ _

Puzzle #60
BIRTHDAY PARTY

DSAEDSR   _ _ _ _ _ _ _

EBUL   _ _ _ _

EIANCBALP   _ _ _ _ _ _ _ _ _

SOBS   _ _ _ _

UNEITRNGS   _ _ _ _ _ _ _ _ _

DAEL   _ _ _ _

HUCRS   _ _ _ _ _

POEISREM   _ _ _ _ _ _ _ _

FLAEERD   _ _ _ _ _ _ _

TVACAE   _ _ _ _ _ _

HCASRE   _ _ _ _ _ _

RTEOITYANS   _ _ _ _ _ _ _ _ _ _

THSU

_ _ _ _

SROPO

_ _ _ _ _

COAX

_ _ _ _

ORAR

_ _ _ _

ODERR

_ _ _ _ _

EHYPZR

_ _ _ _ _ _

IENYMMLES

_ _ _ _ _ _ _ _ _

EPOSUODNR

_ _ _ _ _ _ _ _ _

OAMPEHTLNY

_ _ _ _ _ _ _ _ _ _

RIVOY

_ _ _ _ _

RTETSOIO

_ _ _ _ _ _ _ _

EFAILNSP

_ _ _ _ _ _ _ _

INTERIOR DESIGN

LWUDNEYI

_ _ _ _ _ _ _ _

EUTEBSVLI

_ _ _ _ _ _ _ _ _

ATTTOO

_ _ _ _ _ _

AROCEONITD

_ _ _ _ _ _ _ _ _ _

SLCLPOA

_ _ _ _ _ _ _

FWILLU

_ _ _ _ _ _

LEPCENTA

_ _ _ _ _ _ _ _

WOELB

_ _ _ _ _

EEMT

_ _ _ _

TEROR

_ _ _ _ _

ESLTIMREAN

_ _ _ _ _ _ _ _ _ _

IFRTTE

_ _ _ _ _ _

SOUP

RCBOSTH _ _ _ _ _ _ _

OTAETGP _ _ _ _ _ _ _

RDWHECO _ _ _ _ _ _ _

TLIT _ _ _ _

ENERTSOIMN _ _ _ _ _ _ _ _ _ _

HTHOHCTCPO _ _ _ _ _ _ _ _ _ _

LTXAIO _ _ _ _ _ _

OPONS _ _ _ _ _

LNRMEATA _ _ _ _ _ _ _ _

ALEK _ _ _ _

INTH _ _ _ _

AJRONLU _ _ _ _ _ _ _

GGOGJNI   _ _ _ _ _ _ _

CELXERECY   _ _ _ _ _ _ _ _ _

LECCMNYE   _ _ _ _ _ _ _ _

EDCRILTNAE   _ _ _ _ _ _ _ _ _ _

NNTEAEITR   _ _ _ _ _ _ _ _ _

METREOADIM   _ _ _ _ _ _ _ _ _ _

OWGL   _ _ _ _

ETITOAMNN   _ _ _ _ _ _ _ _ _

TOHSL   _ _ _ _ _

PNALK   _ _ _ _ _

EROPPSS   _ _ _ _ _ _ _

NETO   _ _ _ _

Puzzle #65
FILM MAKING

SANIEN   _ _ _ _ _ _

IRCLAGNE   _ _ _ _ _ _ _ _

EERD   _ _ _ _

EYCAKR   _ _ _ _ _ _

LBABEB   _ _ _ _ _ _

GILREVANE   _ _ _ _ _ _ _ _ _

STMEOUC   _ _ _ _ _ _ _

EVGLOUERAT   _ _ _ _ _ _ _ _ _ _

RSHEOOT   _ _ _ _ _ _ _

TBNNGIU   _ _ _ _ _ _ _

AGZEU   _ _ _ _ _

TARXE   _ _ _ _ _

MAGIC

MDBIIOLSA   _ _ _ _ _ _ _ _ _

REGLUJG   _ _ _ _ _ _ _

TFNEAIASCD   _ _ _ _ _ _ _ _ _ _

AGBTEETU   _ _ _ _ _ _ _ _

MLEGO   _ _ _ _ _

ABEHO   _ _ _ _ _

MHWMAY   _ _ _ _ _ _

ORUTGMW   _ _ _ _ _ _ _

RAYFI   _ _ _ _ _

TASSRHYOEO   _ _ _ _ _ _ _ _ _ _

NATRLEN   _ _ _ _ _ _ _

EILW   _ _ _ _

AIRPORT

STRDADEN

_ _ _ _ _ _ _ _

CARPOAHP

_ _ _ _ _ _ _ _

REICLMA

_ _ _ _ _ _ _

NHSNONA

_ _ _ _ _ _ _

MEBA

_ _ _ _

NHALED

_ _ _ _ _ _

RRAMOOEED

_ _ _ _ _ _ _ _ _

HETPIRLO

_ _ _ _ _ _ _ _

SLRAMAH

_ _ _ _ _ _ _

EGRBCIDA

_ _ _ _ _ _ _ _

FIENGR

_ _ _ _ _ _

KOSC

_ _ _ _

Puzzle #68
SLEEPING

UELVIIZSA

_ _ _ _ _ _ _ _ _

NAWIOGEBN

_ _ _ _ _ _ _ _ _

ESIFEYLLT

_ _ _ _ _ _ _ _ _

NLAEMDRAD

_ _ _ _ _ _ _ _ _

RVPMEOI

_ _ _ _ _ _ _

DCOA

_ _ _ _

EOLGD

_ _ _ _ _

RNTMODA

_ _ _ _ _ _ _

EAAWK

_ _ _ _ _

NTUINCIOBA

_ _ _ _ _ _ _ _ _ _

TNVSATIOIE

_ _ _ _ _ _ _ _ _ _

EAULPSER

_ _ _ _ _ _ _ _

GRAPHIC DESIGN

NTPRI

_ _ _ _ _

CURNNCEEORC

_ _ _ _ _ _ _ _ _ _ _

SYBU

_ _ _ _

ETIAPGMTE

_ _ _ _ _ _ _ _ _

INVEETINV

_ _ _ _ _ _ _ _ _

DENISEGR

_ _ _ _ _ _ _ _

EIACLTT

_ _ _ _ _ _ _

POCTHOYPO

_ _ _ _ _ _ _ _ _

EPRNEDT

_ _ _ _ _ _ _

BRREMEYDIO

_ _ _ _ _ _ _ _ _ _

KTOESR

_ _ _ _ _ _

HOSEU

_ _ _ _ _

Puzzle #70

WINE

ECLDAN   _ _ _ _ _ _

RREKSPLA   _ _ _ _ _ _ _ _

INCAASNOM   _ _ _ _ _ _ _ _ _

BUHS   _ _ _ _

GREOU   _ _ _ _ _

NTTE   _ _ _ _

SVOUNI   _ _ _ _ _ _

EWRI   _ _ _ _

TAERNIT   _ _ _ _ _ _ _

OGUHR   _ _ _ _ _

QROLIU   _ _ _ _ _ _

ROKNUC   _ _ _ _ _ _

Puzzle #71
WEDDING PLANNING

ENSPCIREEC _ _ _ _ _ _ _ _ _

EUFLELLGY _ _ _ _ _ _ _ _ _

RATCH _ _ _ _ _

PIIECTUPORS _ _ _ _ _ _ _ _ _ _ _

OSAMLROPPA _ _ _ _ _ _ _ _ _ _

CLRTOLRNOE _ _ _ _ _ _ _ _ _ _

TAONBI _ _ _ _ _ _

SSTEPDREAHE _ _ _ _ _ _ _ _ _ _ _

MVOERCEO _ _ _ _ _ _ _ _

ACIAEMTNH _ _ _ _ _ _ _ _ _

VTCORINE _ _ _ _ _ _ _ _

SPAOUEONTNS _ _ _ _ _ _ _ _ _ _ _

NEWS

NMSSERPA

_ _ _ _ _ _ _ _

RSTI

_ _ _ _

NEAROTCTOMM

_ _ _ _ _ _ _ _ _ _ _

EACS

_ _ _ _

VADSI

_ _ _ _ _

OPRTRERE

_ _ _ _ _ _ _ _

OCNU

_ _ _ _

AREANCG

_ _ _ _ _ _ _

SUULTETBTCT

_ _ _ _ _ _ _ _ _ _ _

PNADME

_ _ _ _ _ _

LSDEPEA

_ _ _ _ _ _ _

ENONWMWSA

_ _ _ _ _ _ _ _ _

HEALTH

NETVOOID

_ _ _ _ _ _ _ _

MTRI

_ _ _ _

EONUCB

_ _ _ _ _ _

TIOPPT

_ _ _ _ _ _

TAPNPTANRUE

_ _ _ _ _ _ _ _ _ _ _

BESSL

_ _ _ _ _

NIICRGLPP

_ _ _ _ _ _ _ _ _

HTEYRA

_ _ _ _ _ _

USHC

_ _ _ _

EHTBA

_ _ _ _ _

LNILCICA

_ _ _ _ _ _ _ _

ERTIRE

_ _ _ _ _ _

BSLASOTAR

_ _ _ _ _ _ _ _ _

EWAK

_ _ _ _

CINISOAMRE

_ _ _ _ _ _ _ _ _ _

GNHAHASI

_ _ _ _ _ _ _ _

AOWHO

_ _ _ _ _

PNSTOTEEC

_ _ _ _ _ _ _ _ _

OCBAI

_ _ _ _ _

RVNAOVECU

_ _ _ _ _ _ _ _ _

LEOITLALWY

_ _ _ _ _ _ _ _ _ _

TUBA

_ _ _ _

IMLA

_ _ _ _

HELEODSHAV

_ _ _ _ _ _ _ _ _ _

Puzzle #75
RESTAURANT

SREERVE   _ _ _ _ _ _ _

UBLEUHCOS   _ _ _ _ _ _ _ _ _

GISMKON   _ _ _ _ _ _ _

TARS   _ _ _ _

OHTS   _ _ _ _

ROSEC   _ _ _ _ _

PEHL   _ _ _ _

ADLY   _ _ _ _

SHCIARE   _ _ _ _ _ _ _

LEDWL   _ _ _ _ _

RASWOHMO   _ _ _ _ _ _ _ _

RSUOC   _ _ _ _ _

Puzzle #76
GERMANY

SEAPTOG   _ _ _ _ _ _ _

UHEENZAKKR   _ _ _ _ _ _ _ _ _ _

BERST   _ _ _ _ _

TLUNADJ   _ _ _ _ _ _ _

CSHUF   _ _ _ _ _

EARGVMRA   _ _ _ _ _ _ _ _

OARBN   _ _ _ _ _

ARMK   _ _ _ _

NGMARE   _ _ _ _ _ _

IMCSEAU   _ _ _ _ _ _ _

ALLTREEKHSR   _ _ _ _ _ _ _ _ _ _

CELAAS   _ _ _ _ _ _

URBAN FARMING

YRCUTS

_ _ _ _ _ _

REAA

_ _ _ _

UAVCTDTLIE

_ _ _ _ _ _ _ _ _ _

ORRAWH

_ _ _ _ _ _

ULENTN

_ _ _ _ _ _

LCGIKROD

_ _ _ _ _ _ _ _

ALREBA

_ _ _ _ _ _

PORO

_ _ _ _

LLMA

_ _ _ _

BTLE

_ _ _ _

ARBIOR

_ _ _ _ _ _

OISL

_ _ _ _

PREGNANCY

ETTCNRUEDOP   _ _ _ _ _ _ _ _ _ _

GATNADOIVIR   _ _ _ _ _ _ _ _ _ _

ONREAEMHARO   _ _ _ _ _ _ _ _ _ _

ARLOM   _ _ _ _ _

CILOPMEOAH   _ _ _ _ _ _ _ _ _ _

NEUCKIQ   _ _ _ _ _ _ _

DQAU   _ _ _ _

EANTOITNMIR   _ _ _ _ _ _ _ _ _ _ _

IRTEOCBTS   _ _ _ _ _ _ _ _ _

BTLUA   _ _ _ _ _

IPAC   _ _ _ _

RIEACPATCML   _ _ _ _ _ _ _ _ _ _ _

Puzzle #79
SILENT MOVIES

NTROPOLO   _ _ _ _ _ _ _ _

KPIS   _ _ _ _

IEGILANNBT   _ _ _ _ _ _ _ _ _ _

LAML   _ _ _ _

TNEHIATOIS   _ _ _ _ _ _ _ _ _ _

RGENDE   _ _ _ _ _ _

SRSCHONPIE   _ _ _ _ _ _ _ _ _ _

IEESSLNOS   _ _ _ _ _ _ _ _ _

EDOCVI   _ _ _ _ _ _

KTRE   _ _ _ _

IFLL   _ _ _ _

STLEUCT   _ _ _ _ _ _ _

USRYYP   _ _ _ _ _ _

AABDLROE   _ _ _ _ _ _ _ _

CATFEF   _ _ _ _ _ _

ANOTTNCS   _ _ _ _ _ _ _ _

DPRIPY   _ _ _ _ _ _

SCROS   _ _ _ _ _

SPOTUPR   _ _ _ _ _ _ _

EESVR   _ _ _ _ _

HDTHBOEORRO   _ _ _ _ _ _ _ _ _ _ _

TEESEWI   _ _ _ _ _ _ _

YARLIBDD   _ _ _ _ _ _ _ _

NOOSP   _ _ _ _ _

Puzzle #81

SOLDIER

CSACKOS   _ _ _ _ _ _ _

RCELNA   _ _ _ _ _ _

COTSU   _ _ _ _ _

ESETDR   _ _ _ _ _ _

ATEFREULD   _ _ _ _ _ _ _ _ _

DNDBAIS   _ _ _ _ _ _ _

EALRTTB   _ _ _ _ _ _ _

RDTAECO   _ _ _ _ _ _ _

EBOORK   _ _ _ _ _ _

EICNITZ   _ _ _ _ _ _ _

IILFUSER   _ _ _ _ _ _ _ _

AHWESROR   _ _ _ _ _ _ _ _

LNISPDDCIIE   _ _ _ _ _ _ _ _ _ _ _

LLUIINOS   _ _ _ _ _ _ _ _

MLSUP   _ _ _ _ _

UATRQ   _ _ _ _ _

RLAEFWE   _ _ _ _ _ _ _

EOBNARERICT   _ _ _ _ _ _ _ _ _ _ _

HCYEGNII   _ _ _ _ _ _ _ _

DEHA   _ _ _ _

EFTELT   _ _ _ _ _ _

TMEENTTRA   _ _ _ _ _ _ _ _ _

NSUCEUTLC   _ _ _ _ _ _ _ _ _

MLORNA   _ _ _ _ _ _

ANT

LCNOIMPAE   _ _ _ _ _ _ _ _ _

OYRFIARCM   _ _ _ _ _ _ _ _ _

ORWEKR   _ _ _ _ _ _

LUBODLG   _ _ _ _ _ _ _

HLIL   _ _ _ _

ANSATIASL   _ _ _ _ _ _ _ _ _

NYONGOYM   _ _ _ _ _ _ _ _

ERUEPRNNTAO   _ _ _ _ _ _ _ _ _ _ _

AMROAITN   _ _ _ _ _ _ _ _

IPAMSBHAAEN   _ _ _ _ _ _ _ _ _ _ _

NUDMATAA   _ _ _ _ _ _ _ _

ECLIDPE   _ _ _ _ _ _ _

TREE

TAAP　　　　　　　_ _ _ _

RALOPP　　　　　　_ _ _ _ _ _

SATEMM　　　　　　_ _ _ _ _ _

NAMEORNT　　　　　_ _ _ _ _ _ _ _

AASANCRD　　　　　_ _ _ _ _ _ _ _

TSINAR　　　　　　_ _ _ _ _ _

OBRS　　　　　　　_ _ _ _

BLRIFTE　　　　　　_ _ _ _ _ _ _

PHCEA　　　　　　　_ _ _ _ _

DLAESDT　　　　　　_ _ _ _ _ _ _

ODAWLODNSA　　　　_ _ _ _ _ _ _ _ _ _

ANAMYOB　　　　　　_ _ _ _ _ _ _

Puzzle #85
VALUE OF TIME

ILHWE   _ _ _ _ _

MIEPR   _ _ _ _ _

IECIPFCS   _ _ _ _ _ _ _ _

ITGLHF   _ _ _ _ _ _

ROLL   _ _ _ _

NEDEEPNTD   _ _ _ _ _ _ _ _ _

MNIIM   _ _ _ _ _

NRNOALTEMA   _ _ _ _ _ _ _ _ _ _

FTNIYNII   _ _ _ _ _ _ _ _

YTASHR   _ _ _ _ _ _

IAZLEIIINT   _ _ _ _ _ _ _ _ _ _

NCOIRIDTA   _ _ _ _ _ _ _ _ _

Puzzle #86
WILD

OANNWT   _ _ _ _ _ _

GLRAAARW   _ _ _ _ _ _ _ _

ARFASI   _ _ _ _ _ _

MNTAHI   _ _ _ _ _ _

EFLL   _ _ _ _

ETROCV   _ _ _ _ _ _

EMALTMR   _ _ _ _ _ _ _ _

PHEES   _ _ _ _ _

EHISRK   _ _ _ _ _ _

EKLA   _ _ _ _

VELUTTCIA   _ _ _ _ _ _ _ _ _ _

CEIERF   _ _ _ _ _ _

Puzzle #87
VIOLIN LESSONS

TAEK _ _ _ _

BUEDSISA _ _ _ _ _ _ _ _

ODNECS _ _ _ _ _ _

IARYF _ _ _ _ _

OFMRLREY _ _ _ _ _ _ _ _

TOROVSIU _ _ _ _ _ _ _ _

EGRB _ _ _ _

SLSLUYBA _ _ _ _ _ _ _ _

DPTERUNAA _ _ _ _ _ _ _ _ _

ARSPEC _ _ _ _ _ _

IEACTLR _ _ _ _ _ _ _

COSANSNEDI _ _ _ _ _ _ _ _ _ _

Puzzle #88
CONCERT

OCIETNRSDC   _ _ _ _ _ _ _ _ _ _

GUTCINT   _ _ _ _ _ _ _

ETCBSKAGA   _ _ _ _ _ _ _ _ _

NELGAW   _ _ _ _ _ _

RMAWS   _ _ _ _ _

ASET   _ _ _ _

NEILLBGEIG   _ _ _ _ _ _ _ _ _ _

EGAT   _ _ _ _

ONAMSISDI   _ _ _ _ _ _ _ _ _

BOTEGLO   _ _ _ _ _ _ _

HCLOAR   _ _ _ _ _ _

WALZT   _ _ _ _ _

ENVIRONMENT POLLUTIO

BOACNIUTR   _ _ _ _ _ _ _ _ _

CNONTOXI   _ _ _ _ _ _ _ _

ATEWAYG   _ _ _ _ _ _ _

NTSIITORNA   _ _ _ _ _ _ _ _ _ _ _

KNOWNUN   _ _ _ _ _ _ _

EGLIOTNAUR   _ _ _ _ _ _ _ _ _ _

EHSICPO   _ _ _ _ _ _ _

EATOLIGB   _ _ _ _ _ _ _ _

AEYBRSPECC   _ _ _ _ _ _ _ _ _ _

ENGRE   _ _ _ _ _

NERASGTR   _ _ _ _ _ _ _ _

BRSCEBRU   _ _ _ _ _ _ _ _

Puzzle #90
RUGBY

CAYHR   _ _ _ _ _

TNSIHASG   _ _ _ _ _ _ _ _

DSHIEL   _ _ _ _ _ _

RDWESDA   _ _ _ _ _ _ _

OLOLATBF   _ _ _ _ _ _ _ _

PROP   _ _ _ _

RUEGRG   _ _ _ _ _ _

SPRIPEMIHRE   _ _ _ _ _ _ _ _ _ _ _

FOAYR   _ _ _ _ _

OSNENOIRCV   _ _ _ _ _ _ _ _ _ _

MEAL   _ _ _ _

CALHT   _ _ _ _ _

Puzzle #91
SHIRT

NDTRSIWBA

_ _ _ _ _ _ _ _ _

NKECITE

_ _ _ _ _ _ _

AONMOR

_ _ _ _ _ _

ELOTCGAEEDL

_ _ _ _ _ _ _ _ _ _ _

APOINERF

_ _ _ _ _ _ _ _

LMBEPRAEE

_ _ _ _ _ _ _ _ _

DLUO

_ _ _ _

VERRDOSES

_ _ _ _ _ _ _ _ _

MTLEICOPEN

_ _ _ _ _ _ _ _ _ _

LGYIPMS

_ _ _ _ _ _ _

WPITANTAYS

_ _ _ _ _ _ _ _ _ _

DLBIAGIAR

_ _ _ _ _ _ _ _ _

ADEAH   _ _ _ _ _

ELDEUSCH   _ _ _ _ _ _ _ _

YADWRKO   _ _ _ _ _ _ _

DSOHRVEETI   _ _ _ _ _ _ _ _ _ _

RAEFI   _ _ _ _ _

KWWROEKE   _ _ _ _ _ _ _ _

TAUEYSD   _ _ _ _ _ _ _

SRCHETT   _ _ _ _ _ _ _

OCSEL   _ _ _ _ _

TRIW   _ _ _ _

RTFEOLVSE   _ _ _ _ _ _ _ _ _

OTORRP   _ _ _ _ _ _

KUCD

DIERPP

CESYPAAHTHB

USPM

HGYCTOIOLHY

PUASC

CIBAKHDC

MUJP

HHEPYTERASB

GNAENT

LNFOCA

PERLET

NVIALARC _ _ _ _ _ _ _ _

ALED _ _ _ _

HMOS _ _ _ _

RAVE _ _ _ _

ATSXFRIN _ _ _ _ _ _ _ _

SEEIPRXET _ _ _ _ _ _ _ _ _

RIQUDLEAL _ _ _ _ _ _ _ _ _

ABAMS _ _ _ _ _

RPTI _ _ _ _

ERANMG _ _ _ _ _ _

SLASA _ _ _ _ _

EEUROPTTI _ _ _ _ _ _ _ _ _

WORLD

RNCNUIEANT _ _ _ _ _ _ _ _ _

AORNGNE _ _ _ _ _ _ _

IWDODLEWR _ _ _ _ _ _ _ _ _

VIWE _ _ _ _

CELPA _ _ _ _ _

SELME _ _ _ _ _

EIRSA _ _ _ _ _

ERISPHBEO _ _ _ _ _ _ _ _ _

ONLIITATRSE _ _ _ _ _ _ _ _ _ _ _

AKRCC _ _ _ _ _

SWET _ _ _ _

PLNNEOMEAH _ _ _ _ _ _ _ _ _ _

Puzzle #96
ONLINE SHOPPING

CIIZTEN   _ _ _ _ _ _ _

PCOUNO   _ _ _ _ _ _

NAOHRC   _ _ _ _ _ _

ETKBAS   _ _ _ _ _ _

FEDE   _ _ _ _

TPLA   _ _ _ _

TPOS   _ _ _ _

LANHED   _ _ _ _ _ _

OYVENRTNI   _ _ _ _ _ _ _ _ _

LMLA   _ _ _ _

ZGAER   _ _ _ _ _

NRORTCBUIOT   _ _ _ _ _ _ _ _ _ _ _

Puzzle #97
PHOTO EDITING

RDOOREFPA   _ _ _ _ _ _ _ _ _

TDOMENEANI   _ _ _ _ _ _ _ _ _ _

IDTE   _ _ _ _

ARIBB   _ _ _ _ _

IBANYEVTLI   _ _ _ _ _ _ _ _ _ _

TEFYININS   _ _ _ _ _ _ _ _ _

GRNIMTMI   _ _ _ _ _ _ _ _

APACBKY   _ _ _ _ _ _ _

EPNO   _ _ _ _

CATCH   _ _ _ _ _

SRPAH   _ _ _ _ _

UONFDRGEOR   _ _ _ _ _ _ _ _ _ _

Puzzle #98
HEALTHY SNACKS

COENGONE

_ _ _ _ _ _ _ _

VGIRUO

_ _ _ _ _ _

TREYUBT

_ _ _ _ _ _ _

ORATWHRME

_ _ _ _ _ _ _ _ _

LIHA

_ _ _ _

ISEASRDHN

_ _ _ _ _ _ _ _ _

IDRECIOP

_ _ _ _ _ _ _ _

AEUNMR

_ _ _ _ _ _

TLAOL

_ _ _ _ _

RUNPE

_ _ _ _ _

CSIESIMTO

_ _ _ _ _ _ _ _ _

EMEIRG

_ _ _ _ _ _

Puzzle #99
RAINBOW

ERLSSUL   _ _ _ _ _ _ _

GYDUA   _ _ _ _ _

INOPAEL   _ _ _ _ _ _ _

DAGSAR   _ _ _ _ _ _

YIPT   _ _ _ _

UPPGY   _ _ _ _ _

OVNIIITECVS   _ _ _ _ _ _ _ _ _ _ _

GUODNS   _ _ _ _ _ _

TDEEIRNICS   _ _ _ _ _ _ _ _ _ _

USCTPREM   _ _ _ _ _ _ _ _

MLDLEAHI   _ _ _ _ _ _ _ _

TAAPRGNEY   _ _ _ _ _ _ _ _ _

Puzzle #100
SWIMMING

HREO

_ _ _ _

SERESNA

_ _ _ _ _ _ _

VOTIRGE

_ _ _ _ _ _ _

IKIBIN

_ _ _ _ _ _

LMEVU

_ _ _ _ _

OPLHSAEYR

_ _ _ _ _ _ _ _ _

MWEMRTSIE

_ _ _ _ _ _ _ _ _

OSEGO

_ _ _ _ _

RTPNIAEDUO

_ _ _ _ _ _ _ _ _ _

OCTIMSHXEA

_ _ _ _ _ _ _ _ _ _

LSPA

_ _ _ _

GINW

_ _ _ _

SUMMER

LROFOPFOO = FOOLPROOF

NEEERGVRE = EVERGREEN

NOIACNT = CONTAIN

ALUNLYNA = ANNUALLY

CRDU = CRUD

ZOLCA = COLZA

UFEMERP = PERFUME

BNCAI = CABIN

FDIEINNG = DEFINING

TOATS = STOAT

IAINNKNM = MANNIKIN

SSEOOUS = OSSEOUS

Puzzle # 2
MAGIC TRICKS

ANTATR = TANTRA

RGMOUWT = MUGWORT

LOTCUC = OCCULT

REOOCJTRP = PROJECTOR

DERSUC = CURSED

RRCNJUOO = CONJUROR

IHLBDRUN = BRUNHILD

OJEUNCR = CONJURE

ROUNCYJ = CONJURY

EXIPI = PIXIE

DAMZEA = AMAZED

RCAHM = CHARM

Puzzle # 3
COMIC BOOKS

IOSCNOTTAR = CARTOONIST

MCLFIOMIR = MICROFILM

HCRALSO = SCHOLAR

ASGET = STAGE

RIANRBILA = LIBRARIAN

EEEOKPBOKR = BOOKKEEPER

KSMDAA = DAMASK

PROM = ROMP

NUDRO = ROUND

PCONSIROMA = COMPARISON

RPTTAE = PATTER

TBLIEGR = GILBERT

Puzzle # 4
FUNNY

YHIRATLI   =   HILARITY

QPUI   =   QUIP

AEOPTNTYLIL   =   POTENTIALLY

IWYMSH   =   WHIMSY

LFACIRCA   =   FARCICAL

EITTAUTNONA   =   ATTENUATION

HSCU   =   SUCH

YPROAD   =   PARODY

ABDARTS   =   BASTARD

IMCNYAD   =   DYNAMIC

NICCEKH   =   CHICKEN

SFCEE   =   FECES

MODEL TRAINS

DREVI	=	DRIVE
CCREROT	=	CORRECT
TMOAHPN	=	PHANTOM
SPHEOWEP	=	PEEPSHOW
MRNHAOSE	=	HORSEMAN
LACSE	=	SCALE
UACCARCY	=	ACCURACY
TNEROM	=	MENTOR
TTUPICAYLNU	=	PUNCTUALITY
EGRFROE	=	REFORGE
RAYLTEAHCP	=	ARCHETYPAL
OYRMFITCNO	=	CONFORMITY

MAIL

ERABTE = REBATE

YAST = STAY

DUAFR = FRAUD

TNEIND = INTEND

EGSA = SAGE

ODNDLLAR = LANDLORD

ERRVSE = SERVER

AFROG = FARGO

EGTLUANT = GAUNTLET

CTAATSROINN = TRANSACTION

ERIALT = RETAIL

PSOT = POST

ETIMRS = MISTER

EATNRIUIM = MINIATURE

RIMIVTIPE = PRIMITIVE

NAFYC = FANCY

HATICRLAET = THEATRICAL

ETEAHRT = THEATER

TURVSOOI = VIRTUOSO

ARENYNT = TANNERY

PLTETAE = PALETTE

MOIID = IDIOM

CPRACETI = PRACTICE

UPSO = OPUS

Puzzle # 8

MONEY

LLASM	=	SMALL
LIOUDIQANTI	=	LIQUIDATION
TOLO	=	LOOT
UUYRS	=	USURY
KOOH	=	HOOK
EKIT	=	KITE
RTAEBR	=	BARTER
TSNMISA	=	SANTIMS
VSNGAI	=	SAVING
HCEESE	=	CHEESE
LRNDEE	=	LENDER
UOSTMC	=	CUSTOM

STAMP COLLECTING

PITNMRI = IMPRINT

HEAURSRGC = SURCHARGE

REDNESCNO = CONDENSER

VARGE = GRAVE

OCLAIONTL = COLLATION

NTLIPGA = PLATING

TNHYOLAOG = ANTHOLOGY

ORIOTC = OCTROI

PRNOEUD = POUNDER

LMLI = MILL

LIEHIILBBPO = BIBLIOPHILE

VREMESPIIS = IMPRESSIVE

Puzzle # 10
FASHION

HOKO	=	HOOK
HCLEE	=	LEECH
MILYTE	=	TIMELY
RSTELPSETER	=	LETTERPRESS
EEROPTTL	=	TELEPORT
NDGILOME	=	MODELING
MLUBEM	=	MUMBLE
TTTIRABUE	=	ATTRIBUTE
RFMNIO	=	INFORM
GSDSEOD	=	GODDESS
ALMBRCSE	=	SCRAMBLE
EAKTS	=	SKATE

Puzzle # 11

BOUNDARIES

TMMENNOU	=	MONUMENT
RLAI	=	RAIL
TPIRCENC	=	PRECINCT
YARLIIL	=	ILLYRIA
EIANFEDBL	=	DEFINABLE
VIOIONTAL	=	VIOLATION
OANTICID	=	DIATONIC
NMELAIFT	=	FILAMENT
ECPRNISOSO	=	PROCESSION
BONUD	=	BOUND
CODIFNUNEN	=	UNCONFINED
RVSEYU	=	SURVEY

Puzzle # 12
ORIGINAL

EANR	=	NEAR
RPSTI	=	STRIP
IANCTT	=	INTACT
ENEIMPERTX	=	EXPERIMENT
TRRUCOP	=	CORRUPT
OERAMETSL	=	ELASTOMER
YCIADNM	=	DYNAMIC
OGWR	=	GROW
RDFOEM	=	DEFORM
TRKSDICAE	=	SIDETRACK
TITWS	=	TWIST
ERTEVPDER	=	PERVERTED

Puzzle # 13
WOMEN EMPOWERMENT

ANSOPRO = SOPRANO

DERSUT = DUSTER

OSYNIOSMGU = MISOGYNOUS

MLCTICCAREI = CLIMACTERIC

SEXISM = SEXISM

AUKBR = BURKA

LFOW = FLOW

YNSIMOIGSM = MISOGYNISM

OAPCBM = MOBCAP

RSEREIBAS = BRASSIERE

MSIMIFNE = FEMINISM

PEMRUTC = CRUMPET

TIME MANAGEMENT

STAIENCN = INSTANCE

ASSEPAG = PASSAGE

ESBOILEPNRS = RESPONSIBLE

TSMOHRE = SMOTHER

NNGINUR = RUNNING

ICUAGOSSA = SAGACIOUS

IJFYF = JIFFY

TTNAARCS = TRANSACT

FIYRLBE = BRIEFLY

EUTTPR = PUTTER

ESGPAPOT = STOPPAGE

TLTLEI = LITTLE

PERSONAL FINANCE

HCOTU = TOUCH

SPEAATER = SEPARATE

VUREEEN = REVENUE

WATN = WANT

IARSAMCH = CHARISMA

RBELLIA = LIBERAL

REARIFM = FIREARM

AGMTZEIEN = MAGNETIZE

EITRLECD = DERELICT

AIFSONH = FASHION

TIBERM = TIMBER

RCEONR = CORNER

GARDEN

OBMCXOC = COXCOMB

TSKOC = STOCK

CREA = CARE

EGSLOASUSH = GLASSHOUSE

EEBNTN = BENNET

EREARTC = TERRACE

PAGDOA = PAGODA

PNOE = OPEN

RLYEGLA = GALLERY

RYRCKOE = ROCKERY

BDNRA = BRAND

TSPE = PEST

Puzzle # 17

NUTRITION

LORATTUININ	=	NUTRITIONAL
URNSE	=	NURSE
ERTHEROOPHT	=	HETEROTROPH
JEEJNU	=	JEJUNE
CONNTIFU	=	FUNCTION
PANS	=	SNAP
OTAAIIXTNND	=	ANTIOXIDANT
IALYROOGGBO	=	AGROBIOLOGY
SIHTARIC	=	RACHITIS
ETEIDICT	=	DIETETIC
CUFENI	=	UNICEF
ORIOSSHCL	=	CHLOROSIS

Puzzle # 18
BASKETBALL

BREUNDO	=	REBOUND
GITVIOMATN	=	MOTIVATING
VALTREYIITS	=	VERSATILITY
OPST	=	POST
DOHAWDRO	=	HARDWOOD
ICNIVOTNAO	=	INVOCATION
ETLGA	=	AGLET
EDFT	=	DEFT
MIITGNDNAO	=	DOMINATING
LCOANTIOSNO	=	CONSOLATION
YTIINIBAL	=	INABILITY
RCTNOEV	=	CONVERT

CHINA

OOBACTC = TOBACCO

IAEELGW = WEIGELA

OMSRMASCI = COMMISSAR

NSAI = SIAN

HNLOAWC = LANCHOW

ONGKME = MEKONG

KWANNTUGG = KWANGTUNG

EBIHE = HEBEI

ULPIC = PICUL

DLALRO = DOLLAR

OXERB = BOXER

BCSAAU = ABACUS

Puzzle # 20
GAME

WTTIERS	=	TWISTER
OTIPN	=	POINT
LEDA	=	DEAL
YKPO	=	POKY
CILK	=	LICK
VRKEEO	=	REVOKE
WRENIN	=	WINNER
OOAHW	=	WAHOO
EBDIGR	=	BRIDGE
SKEAT	=	STAKE
IZQU	=	QUIZ
MCAP	=	CAMP

MONKEY

ABOONB	=	BABOON
INPRAMISO	=	PROSIMIAN
YNGEMBAA	=	MANGABEY
UMKS	=	MUSK
TEERPYRSB	=	PRESBYTER
ESRECS	=	RECESS
ERLAY	=	RELAY
AYRAMNAA	=	RAMAYANA
SBRSA	=	BRASS
OURCIUS	=	CURIOUS
OUSIPELR	=	PERILOUS
TNEUPA	=	PEANUT

Puzzle # 22
FRUGAL LIVING

RITESEL = STERILE

LEUSNITACR = LACUSTRINE

WGLLNDIE = DWELLING

MTLTOEA = MATTOLE

FWERELA = WELFARE

ICHTP = PITCH

AGHROPNEA = ORPHANAGE

TOTNCINSSE = CONSISTENT

STUADETI = SITUATED

OHSEU = HOUSE

CHZEC = CZECH

AHNIAAGN = GHANAIAN

HOTEL

ARNIINTTE	=	ITINERANT
EEPK	=	KEEP
AAGROENPT	=	PATRONAGE
AEFC	=	CAFE
MOAND	=	NOMAD
POLEEERHTKE	=	HOTELKEEPER
DRERI	=	RIDER
BEHPLOL	=	BELLHOP
ORTEPR	=	PORTER
SYPGESAWAA	=	PASSAGEWAY
RGDNA	=	GRAND
SANERGSAME	=	MANAGERESS

POTTERY

UNERNR	=	RUNNER
BTALOL	=	BALLOT
EIENFAC	=	FAIENCE
OMNRSIMEI	=	IMMERSION
ACYL	=	CLAY
GEETRAWAA	=	AGATEWARE
RWEAVEON	=	OVENWARE
NLGALAI	=	GALLINA
HATCW	=	WATCH
ALTME	=	METAL
TDEMTA	=	MATTED
INPYDLO	=	DIPYLON

Puzzle # 25

STRING ART

ANNLTUGE	=	UNTANGLE
OEYTHR	=	THEORY
EFTR	=	FRET
TETLAR	=	RATTLE
RACTECAUIR	=	CARICATURE
CRIDROP	=	RIPCORD
ITAVOANI	=	AVIATION
AGSCSYNTMI	=	GYMNASTICS
MILEUSASRR	=	SURREALISM
NIEL	=	LINE
LEKI	=	LIKE
LIEDRSLITY	=	DISTILLERY

TABLE TENNIS

AOCNN	=	CANON
IEINTS	=	SENITI
TWROH	=	THROW
CASLCSI	=	CLASSIC
GEELDN	=	LEGEND
PFLA	=	FLAP
EAYRPL	=	REPLAY
AIARN	=	NAIRA
YROHNOCGOL	=	CHRONOLOGY
SHAUSQ	=	SQUASH
YISTX	=	SIXTY
YHERCR	=	CHERRY

GERMAN SHEPHERD

ORMST	=	STORM
DGIAD	=	GADDI
TLOLRE	=	TOLLER
UCRELNE	=	LUCERNE
NEILAADHN	=	HANDELIAN
KEZKNEUHAR	=	HAKENKREUZ
EHRHSSEDPES	=	SHEPHERDESS
EUNADB	=	DANUBE
ERANNGNEBT	=	TANNENBERG
RHDEER	=	HERDER
TAORSP	=	PASTOR
REPDEHSH	=	SHEPHERD

FRUIT

GEEDRA = DRAGEE

EPSEYL = SLEEPY

TOOTAM = TOMATO

EIMLY = LIMEY

MEAFEL = FEMALE

ALBBMRE = BRAMBLE

UHIORSS = SOURISH

EYRRETAB = TEABERRY

TOMIFC = COMFIT

HLOETACTR = CHARLOTTE

IINORUTF = FRUITION

AANILVL = VANILLA

Puzzle # 29
ANTI AGING

TEUBEMOANN	=	NABUMETONE
EALD	=	LEAD
ATOCBTINII	=	ANTIBIOTIC
SOTLLEFAR	=	FORESTALL
CAVROEUSDA	=	CADAVEROUS
STRUC	=	CRUST
UBNLT	=	BLUNT
NEIRP	=	RIPEN
ALICV	=	CAVIL
JKILLYO	=	KILLJOY
EOSNEIDPRN	=	PREDNISONE
UBREMALL	=	UMBRELLA

Puzzle # 30
PUZZLE

ICAHGLNEGNL	=	CHALLENGING
EOPRHT	=	POTHER
YCAHTC	=	CATCHY
ZUQI	=	QUIZ
ESLBACRB	=	SCRABBLE
TAENLGNE	=	ENTANGLE
OMDFBUDUN	=	DUMBFOUND
CNTNOCE	=	CONNECT
NAEEBT	=	BEATEN
CITSK	=	STICK
UERQE	=	QUEER
WREDNNTOME	=	WONDERMENT

COPNYA = CANOPY

IOCTLOP = COPILOT

UCPAATLT = CATAPULT

NEEUPDSRGDO = GROUNDSPEED

ONPAR = APRON

MNITEUTRNS = INSTRUMENT

NACDRA = CANARD

UFEL = FUEL

BRAADO = ABOARD

EHLD = HELD

YARAIW = AIRWAY

UOCTNWOHD = TOUCHDOWN

WORKING

OREUTR	=	ROUTER
LSWAOLW	=	SWALLOW
THNGLIGI	=	LIGHTING
TUOVENLIO	=	EVOLUTION
NIUAFPL	=	PAINFUL
RNYYGES	=	SYNERGY
LTSPI	=	SPLIT
PTREAIV	=	PRIVATE
CRSTEE	=	SECRET
GRNENIGINEE	=	ENGINEERING
OHVRITSEG	=	OVERSIGHT
NKAB	=	BANK

POTATO

MRUHPY	=	MURPHY
NOMLUSA	=	SOLANUM
COTQETREU	=	CROQUETTE
OGSCRNSE	=	CONGRESS
TOAR	=	TARO
NEILNMA	=	MELANIN
UBRTE	=	TUBER
TTTYA	=	TATTY
LFTALHUEH	=	HEALTHFUL
EARHCUHA	=	HUARACHE
NSIEDI	=	INSIDE
LIPE	=	PILE

STAR

RYRSAT	=	STARRY
MGAI	=	MAGI
TLASTRE	=	STARLET
DWRAF	=	DWARF
DOURCEVAAS	=	CADAVEROUS
AFRESLOTRW	=	STARFLOWER
ILURSNAG	=	SINGULAR
TGYLEOVIN	=	LONGEVITY
HAORNPAA	=	ANAPHORA
EOMBIROLA	=	BLOOMERIA
MRYELE	=	MERELY
IEETGRSP	=	PRESTIGE

Puzzle # 35
SUPER CAR

EOECRDNSN   =   CONDENSER

MERDMI   =   DIMMER

NGAF   =   FANG

MRCUB   =   CRUMB

IRGUNNN   =   RUNNING

RHSOACER   =   HORSECAR

OCRADAL   =   CARLOAD

KPRA   =   PARK

RLEDNEI   =   REDLINE

TAACR   =   CARAT

IEOTMV   =   MOTIVE

INMEAHC   =   MACHINE

ORTSCKEP	=	SPROCKET
ETGASRGEE	=	SEGREGATE
TBUE	=	TUBE
ACEL	=	LACE
HRETSFI	=	SHIFTER
NSCGIHCOR	=	SCORCHING
PYCIESF	=	SPECIFY
YCELEXREC	=	EXERCYCLE
CBAEDRI	=	CARBIDE
PMDEO	=	MOPED
BTMOOIRKE	=	MOTORBIKE
IRMLOTEMEE	=	MILEOMETER

Puzzle # 37
KNITTING

GLEAYR   =   ARGYLE

OMSMYISPU   =   SYMPOSIUM

CERDAESE   =   DECREASE

ETUSRU   =   SUTURE

ETRTPUM   =   TRUMPET

ARICBF   =   FABRIC

EELNDE   =   NEEDLE

REIONM   =   MERINO

MHRAISFNE   =   FISHERMAN

STTCIH   =   STITCH

CIOTRT   =   TRICOT

EXTTLEI   =   TEXTILE

Puzzle # 38
PEOPLE

SCOENH	=	CHOSEN
RMRUUO	=	RUMOUR
ATEHR	=	EARTH
ECNOREF	=	ENFORCE
YTCONU	=	COUNTY
DEAG	=	AGED
RAWNNDA	=	RWANDAN
ENORARWIPB	=	BRAINPOWER
ACUUIDOSA	=	AUDACIOUS
ENMYE	=	ENEMY
KONNW	=	KNOWN
ADNGR	=	GRAND

Puzzle # 39
TRAFFIC

LEFERI	=	RELIEF
RTCOASAEL	=	ESCALATOR
LIGLSIAOCT	=	LOGISTICAL
MUDMY	=	DUMMY
EREGESTGA	=	SEGREGATE
ECRINALG	=	CLEARING
EOSFTTML	=	LEFTMOST
OTDOPAF	=	FOOTPAD
PLCOEUT	=	COUPLET
BAKC	=	BACK
NHTE	=	THEN
ALRNS	=	SNARL

FISH

ELTGLU	=	GULLET
NSGUUF	=	FUNGUS
TEIAHBWIT	=	WHITEBAIT
EREDES	=	SEEDER
SIOL	=	SOIL
PEHADHSSEE	=	SHEEPSHEAD
FINRMAG	=	FARMING
WRLRGOE	=	GROWLER
UOHGR	=	ROUGH
CBOIA	=	COBIA
ENIADARM	=	MARINADE
CHEK	=	HECK

PUBLIC

LUPTIP	=	PULPIT
FMAR	=	FARM
CGANHE	=	CHANGE
NDECINTI	=	INCIDENT
EFER	=	FREE
OBOEARNLH	=	HONORABLE
LPEAAC	=	PALACE
RSBIEC	=	SCRIBE
VAWLAO	=	AVOWAL
RCAIELT	=	RECITAL
RAENEDIVLEC	=	DELIVERANCE
IRIUTMRV	=	TRIUMVIR

HOME

TAYS	=	STAY
ISON	=	SION
LBHUME	=	HUMBLE
HNOE	=	HONE
SSREOD	=	DOSSER
UMCEOMT	=	COMMUTE
NUTR	=	TURN
FHEOMOKL	=	HOMEFOLK
ECERHSC	=	SCREECH
IOGWERLNEKT	=	TELEWORKING
EHLOW	=	WHOLE
PTYAR	=	PARTY

IMPORTANCE OF WATER

LIACYLTIRC	=	CRITICALLY
LTYUMIHI	=	HUMILITY
TMEEPL	=	TEMPLE
LRKOEVOO	=	OVERLOOK
UESBACTSN	=	SUBSTANCE
HERE	=	HERE
NAVITLAEUDO	=	DEVALUATION
ALNTREC	=	CENTRAL
IRILPCAPN	=	PRINCIPAL
RTEGSENSA	=	GREATNESS
EBTA	=	BETA
SAOWEHMT	=	SOMEWHAT

WIND SURFING

NKBCIGA	=	BACKING
MIRMRET	=	TRIMMER
ARPVO	=	VAPOR
SFUIRUO	=	FURIOUS
NGHSETTR	=	STRENGTH
IKKC	=	KICK
AWER	=	WEAR
IDNW	=	WIND
TEAS	=	EAST
OLUF	=	FOUL
SLTIOBAA	=	SAILBOAT
LCUR	=	CURL

Puzzle # 45
SOLAR ENERGY

RVEVE	=	VERVE
RAITVAL	=	TRAVAIL
RREENEGTEA	=	REGENERATE
AULEROE	=	AUREOLE
EIBLAETTDI	=	DEBILITATE
OHWUREPOES	=	POWERHOUSE
ETIR	=	TIRE
HLAB	=	BLAH
ARPIRE	=	REPAIR
NQUKECI	=	QUICKEN
NDPSE	=	SPEND
LOWRE	=	LOWER

MOVIE

EFOGNRI = FOREIGN

TISCMSA = MISCAST

TAIEEMN = MATINEE

DCCIEENNY = INDECENCY

NUHNAMTAL = LANTHANUM

IERDIOTNN = RENDITION

LOGEBTO = BOOTLEG

DTATICINO = DICTATION

GPLU = PLUG

EPSYK = PESKY

IPERATMESCE = MASTERPIECE

HWINUDOT = WHODUNIT

Puzzle # 47
TOMATO

FTIRU	=	FRUIT
UCGOMELAA	=	GUACAMOLE
ESKUCR	=	SUCKER
DNRIREG	=	GRINDER
TSEPA	=	PASTE
CMHEAELB	=	BECHAMEL
IDREANLME	=	MADRILENE
OYRG	=	GYRO
ISNPXH	=	SPHINX
LYIHPSAS	=	PHYSALIS
IYSPC	=	SPICY
ALOITTLOM	=	TOMATILLO

Puzzle # 48
FOUNDATION

OCRNAH = ANCHOR

BEAS = BASE

ELATSHSIB = ESTABLISH

NITSEWS = WITNESS

ANVICTAXEO = EXCAVATION

STLOO = STOOL

OGLN = LONG

NISEW = SINEW

OTRO = ROOT

ETPIMEES = EPISTEME

NLSIGE = SINGLE

MMRTAINFE = FIRMAMENT

SHOPPING

PLWSRA = SPRAWL

ORAHNC = ANCHOR

AZALP = PLAZA

TADER = TRADE

WTON = TOWN

RYARH = HARRY

FLOOALTF = FOOTFALL

YDDOW = DOWDY

OEPMEYEL = EMPLOYEE

PEITCDAN = PEDANTIC

AMDI = MAID

TNENOSC = CONSENT

Puzzle # 50
MOBILE

ULINPK   =   UPLINK

DROON   =   DONOR

ECNET   =   CTENE

NSYC   =   SYNC

NSCUIHO   =   CUSHION

TNGAREIMS   =   STREAMING

DDAOIRN   =   ANDROID

PPUIYE   =   YUPPIE

CELAAT   =   ACETAL

TAWH   =   THAW

PNLAT   =   PLANT

CUSD   =   SCUD

RMFORE = FORMER

SNULITTAAR = NATURALIST

PICPAETRETI = PERIPATETIC

IATMSNRO = ROMANIST

OAUDSISUS = ASSIDUOUS

LSCAAIBT = CABALIST

EDNTTUS = STUDENT

RUTTO = TUTOR

STHFIELSS = SHIFTLESS

OATIDIGNNIN = INDIGNATION

YATRTRFENI = FRATERNITY

RPHMOOGNA = MONOGRAPH

Puzzle # 52
DESCRIBE YOURSELF

TOCNEUR	=	RECOUNT
TOTSINA	=	STATION
IFDITENY	=	IDENTIFY
EEATRGAGXE	=	EXAGGERATE
ESESN	=	SENSE
ZINEDMOE	=	DEMONIZE
ESUEEZQ	=	SQUEEZE
EDIPR	=	PRIDE
ERSNCE	=	SCREEN
RSAANSCEU	=	ASSURANCE
UOETLQEN	=	ELOQUENT
HCEESP	=	SPEECH

OFFICE

RLUE = RULE

OLRAYAM = MAYORAL

LSTEEAGHIP = LEGATESHIP

FLLI = FILL

HPEIASHD = HEADSHIP

OGLOM = GLOOM

RATTMOSESP = POSTMASTER

ERHI = HEIR

RMETTERNEI = RETIREMENT

ATYCRRIAPH = PATRIARCHY

VODI = VOID

CAENDMHTET = DETACHMENT

Puzzle # 54
CYBER CRIME

LEFON = FELON

SAUEB = ABUSE

TEMNANCNEEH = ENHANCEMENT

SCIK = SICK

ADIR = RAID

CURNAEYTB = CYBERNAUT

SIYDEACNT = SYNDICATE

UBRLRGA = BURGLAR

ANGG = GANG

NESVGTIETIA = INVESTIGATE

LAUDICIS = SUICIDAL

WETAGAY = GETAWAY

Puzzle # 55
TELEVISION

EECEM = EMCEE

OTAFGEO = FOOTAGE

NDEYCOAUMRT = DOCUMENTARY

CYULBTIPI = PUBLICITY

IERLLF = FILLER

SECASC = ACCESS

GFERFA = GAFFER

RTCESHT = STRETCH

DPEURCRO = PRODUCER

RFOAMT = FORMAT

ENIL = LINE

URAAPETCSCL = SPECTACULAR

Puzzle # 56
BUILDING

OBHRATMO	=	BATHROOM
ILFNOOGR	=	FLOORING
IURMUMBNA	=	MANUBRIUM
VAORLY	=	VOLARY
RIUN	=	RUIN
EWPES	=	SWEEP
ORALMKCOO	=	CLOAKROOM
RSICCU	=	CIRCUS
SACAANDR	=	SANDARAC
IEERGHMAT	=	HERMITAGE
ERGIGYP	=	PIGGERY
ERLSBIT	=	BLISTER

Puzzle # 57

MAKING WINE

INRDK	=	DRINK
TLCIIENDBA	=	INDICTABLE
DBOY	=	BODY
LRAAMSA	=	MARSALA
SRLPGNKAI	=	SPARKLING
GNZAIAM	=	AMAZING
TIPON	=	PINOT
RIOL	=	ROIL
LNNGAEPIL	=	PANELLING
GIRDEGOS	=	DISGORGE
YMYGUZR	=	ZYMURGY
ILSYK	=	SILKY

Puzzle # 58
LITERATURE

ENSIUNRAT	=	SATURNINE
VDAE	=	VEDA
HEETM	=	THEME
XIEND	=	INDEX
LOOIPGYLH	=	PHILOLOGY
REDEAR	=	READER
ICEQRTIU	=	CRITIQUE
DRUE	=	RUDE
OAITQTOUN	=	QUOTATION
NRSASAPSU	=	PARNASSUS
TISRRAUESL	=	SURREALIST
ARRDE	=	DREAR

GIRL EDUCATION

TPOTEACTI	=	PETTICOAT
LWHPE	=	WHELP
IYBDD	=	BIDDY
SDNIEIHF	=	FINISHED
ERIP	=	PERI
PLHSY	=	SYLPH
EVLUA	=	VALUE
CSHOLO	=	SCHOOL
RCTEOJP	=	PROJECT
EDEVIPDR	=	DEPRIVED
CEEATDDU	=	EDUCATED
PMIR	=	PRIM

BIRTHDAY PARTY

DSAEDSR = ADDRESS

EBUL = BLUE

EIANCBALP = INCAPABLE

SOBS = BOSS

UNEITRNGS = INSURGENT

DAEL = LEAD

HUCRS = CRUSH

POEISREM = PROMISEE

FLAEERD = FEDERAL

TVACAE = CAVEAT

HCASRE = SEARCH

RTEOITYANS = STATIONERY

Puzzle # 61
ELEPHANT

THSU   =   TUSH

SROPO   =   SPOOR

COAX   =   COAX

ORAR   =   ROAR

ODERR   =   ORDER

EHYPZR   =   ZEPHYR

IENYMMLES   =   IMMENSELY

EPOSUODNR   =   PONDEROUS

OAMPEHTLNY   =   MENOTYPHLA

RIVOY   =   IVORY

RTETSOIO   =   TORTOISE

EFAILNSP   =   LIFESPAN

INTERIOR DESIGN

LWUDNEYI = UNWIELDY

EUTEBSVLI = VESTIBULE

ATTTOO = TATTOO

AROCEONITD = DECORATION

SLCLPOA = SCALLOP

FWILLU = WILFUL

LEPCENTA = PENTACLE

WOELB = BOWEL

EEMT = MEET

TEROR = RETRO

ESLTIMREAN = STREAMLINE

IFRTTE = FITTER

SOUP

RCBOSTH = BORSCHT

OTAETGP = POTTAGE

RDWHECO = CHOWDER

TLIT = TILT

ENERTSOIMN = MINESTRONE

HTHOHCTCPO = HOTCHPOTCH

LTXAIO = OXTAIL

OPONS = SPOON

LNRMEATA = MATERNAL

ALEK = KALE

INTH = THIN

AJRONLU = JOURNAL

EXERCISE

GGOGJNI	=	JOGGING
CELXERECY	=	EXERCYCLE
LECCMNYE	=	CLEMENCY
EDCRILTNAE	=	CREDENTIAL
NNTEAEITR	=	ENTERTAIN
METREOADIM	=	IMMODERATE
OWGL	=	GLOW
ETITOAMNN	=	MENTATION
TOHSL	=	SLOTH
PNALK	=	PLANK
EROPPSS	=	OPPRESS
NETO	=	TONE

Puzzle # 65

FILM MAKING

SANIEN	=	INSANE
IRCLAGNE	=	CLEARING
EERD	=	REED
EYCAKR	=	CREAKY
LBABEB	=	BABBLE
GILREVANE	=	REVEALING
STMEOUC	=	COSTUME
EVGLOUERAT	=	TRAVELOGUE
RSHEOOT	=	RESHOOT
TBNNGIU	=	BUNTING
AGZEU	=	GAUZE
TARXE	=	EXTRA

MAGIC

MDBIIOLSA = DIABOLISM

REGLUJG = JUGGLER

TFNEAIASCD = FASCINATED

AGBTEETU = BAGUETTE

MLEGO = GOLEM

ABEHO = OBEAH

MHWMAY = WHAMMY

ORUTGMW = MUGWORT

RAYFI = FAIRY

TASSRHYOEO = SOOTHSAYER

NATRLEN = LANTERN

EILW = WILE

AIRPORT

STRDADEN	=	STRANDED
CARPOAHP	=	APPROACH
REICLMA	=	RECLAIM
NHSNONA	=	SHANNON
MEBA	=	BEAM
NHALED	=	HANDLE
RRAMOOEED	=	AERODROME
HETPIRLO	=	HELIPORT
SLRAMAH	=	MARSHAL
EGRBCIDA	=	BIRDCAGE
FIENGR	=	FINGER
KOSC	=	SOCK

Puzzle # 68
SLEEPING

UELVIIZSA	=	VISUALIZE
NAWIOGEBN	=	WINNEBAGO
ESIFEYLLT	=	LIFESTYLE
NLAEMDRAD	=	DREAMLAND
RVPMEOI	=	IMPROVE
DCOA	=	CODA
EOLGD	=	LODGE
RNTMODA	=	DORMANT
EAAWK	=	AWAKE
NTUINCIOBA	=	INCUBATION
TNVSATIOIE	=	ESTIVATION
EAULPSER	=	PLEASURE

Puzzle # 69
GRAPHIC DESIGN

NTPRI	=	PRINT
CURNNCEEORC	=	CONCURRENCE
SYBU	=	BUSY
ETIAPGMTE	=	PEGMATITE
INVEETINV	=	INVENTIVE
DENISEGR	=	REDESIGN
EIACLTT	=	LATTICE
POCTHOYPO	=	PHOTOCOPY
EPRNEDT	=	PRETEND
BRREMEYDIO	=	EMBROIDERY
KTOESR	=	STROKE
HOSEU	=	HOUSE

Puzzle # 70
WINE

ECLDAN = CANDLE

RREKSPLA = SPARKLER

INCAASNOM = MACONNAIS

BUHS = BUSH

GREOU = ROUGE

NTTE = TENT

SVOUNI = VINOUS

EWRI = WIRE

TAERNIT = TERTIAN

OGUHR = ROUGH

QROLIU = LIQUOR

ROKNUC = UNCORK

WEDDING PLANNING

ENSPCIREEC	=	PRESCIENCE
EUFLELLGY	=	GLEEFULLY
RATCH	=	CHART
PIIECTUPORS	=	PRECIPITOUS
OSAMLROPPA	=	MALAPROPOS
CLRTOLRNOE	=	CONTROLLER
TAONBI	=	OBTAIN
SSTEPDREAHE	=	SPREADSHEET
MVOERCEO	=	OVERCOME
ACIAEMTNH	=	MACHINATE
VTCORINE	=	CONTRIVE
SPAOUEONTNS	=	SPONTANEOUS

Puzzle # 72
NEWS

NMSSERPA	=	PRESSMAN
RSTI	=	STIR
NEAROTCTOMM	=	COMMENTATOR
EACS	=	CASE
VADSI	=	DAVIS
OPRTRERE	=	REPORTER
OCNU	=	UNCO
AREANCG	=	CARNAGE
SUULTETBTCT	=	SCUTTLEBUTT
PNADME	=	DAMPEN
LSDEPEA	=	ELAPSED
ENONWMWSA	=	NEWSWOMAN

Puzzle # 73

HEALTH

NETVOOID	=	DEVOTION
MTRI	=	TRIM
EONUCB	=	BOUNCE
TIOPPT	=	TIPTOP
TAPNPTANRUE	=	APPURTENANT
BESSL	=	BLESS
NIICRGLPP	=	CRIPPLING
HTEYRA	=	HEARTY
USHC	=	SUCH
EHTBA	=	BATHE
LNILCICA	=	CLINICAL
ERTIRE	=	RETIRE

PACIFIC

BSLASOTAR = ALBATROSS

EWAK = WAKE

CINISOAMRE = MICRONESIA

GNHAHASI = SHANGHAI

AOWHO = WAHOO

PNSTOTEEC = PENTECOST

OCBAI = COBIA

RVNAOVECU = VANCOUVER

LEOITLALWY = YELLOWTAIL

TUBA = TABU

IMLA = LIMA

HELEODSHAV = SHOVELHEAD

RESTAURANT

SREERVE = RESERVE

UBLEUHCOS = CLUBHOUSE

GISMKON = SMOKING

TARS = STAR

OHTS = HOST

ROSEC = SCORE

PEHL = HELP

ADLY = LADY

SHCIARE = CASHIER

LEDWL = DWELL

RASWOHMO = WASHROOM

RSUOC = SCOUR

Puzzle # 76
GERMANY

SEAPTOG   =   GESTAPO

UHEENZAKKR   =   HAKENKREUZ

BERST   =   BREST

TLUNADJ   =   JUTLAND

CSHUF   =   FUCHS

EARGVMRA   =   MARGRAVE

OARBN   =   BARON

ARMK   =   MARK

NGMARE   =   GERMAN

IMCSEAU   =   CAESIUM

ALLTREEKHSR   =   RATHSKELLER

CELAAS   =   ALSACE

URBAN FARMING

YRCUTS	=	CRUSTY
REAA	=	AREA
UAVCTDTLIE	=	CULTIVATED
ORRAWH	=	HARROW
ULENTN	=	TUNNEL
LCGIKROD	=	GRIDLOCK
ALREBA	=	ARABLE
PORO	=	POOR
LLMA	=	MALL
BTLE	=	BELT
ARBIOR	=	BARRIO
OISL	=	SOIL

Puzzle # 78
PREGNANCY

ETTCNRUEDOP	=	UNPROTECTED
GATNADOIVIR	=	GRAVIDATION
ONREAEMHARO	=	AMENORRHOEA
ARLOM	=	MOLAR
CILOPMEOAH	=	PHOCOMELIA
NEUCKIQ	=	QUICKEN
DQAU	=	QUAD
EANTOITNMIR	=	TERMINATION
IRTEOCBTS	=	OBSTETRIC
BTLUA	=	TUBAL
IPAC	=	PICA
RIEACPATCML	=	MALPRACTICE

SILENT MOVIES

NTROPOLO	=	POLTROON
KPIS	=	SKIP
IEGILANNBT	=	INTANGIBLE
LAML	=	MALL
TNEHIATOIS	=	HESITATION
RGENDE	=	GENDER
SRSCHONPIE	=	CENSORSHIP
IEESSLNOS	=	NOISELESS
EDOCVI	=	VOICED
KTRE	=	TREK
IFLL	=	FILL
STLEUCT	=	SCUTTLE

Puzzle # 80
LOVE

USRYYP	=	SYRUPY
AABDLROE	=	ADORABLE
CATFEF	=	AFFECT
ANOTTNCS	=	CONSTANT
DPRIPY	=	DRIPPY
SCROS	=	CROSS
SPOTUPR	=	SUPPORT
EESVR	=	SERVE
HDTHBOEORRO	=	BROTHERHOOD
TEESEWI	=	SWEETIE
YARLIBDD	=	LADYBIRD
NOOSP	=	SPOON

SOLDIER

CSACKOS	=	COSSACK
RCELNA	=	LANCER
COTSU	=	SCOUT
ESETDR	=	DESERT
ATEFREULD	=	DEFAULTER
DNDBAIS	=	DISBAND
EALRTTB	=	BATTLER
RDTAECO	=	REDCOAT
EBOORK	=	BROOKE
EICNITZ	=	CITIZEN
IILFUSER	=	FUSILIER
AHWESROR	=	WARHORSE

Puzzle # 82
MENTAL HEALTH

LNISPDDCIIE	=	DISCIPLINED
LLUIINOS	=	ILLUSION
MLSUP	=	SLUMP
UATRQ	=	QUART
RLAEFWE	=	WELFARE
EOBNARERICT	=	CEREBRATION
HCYEGNII	=	HYGIENIC
DEHA	=	HEAD
EFTELT	=	FETTLE
TMEENTTRA	=	TREATMENT
NSUCEUTLC	=	SUCCULENT
MLORNA	=	NORMAL

ANT

LCNOIMPAE	=	POLICEMAN
OYRFIARCM	=	FORMICARY
ORWEKR	=	WORKER
LUBODLG	=	BULLDOG
HLIL	=	HILL
ANSATIASL	=	ASSAILANT
NYONGOYM	=	MONOGYNY
ERUEPRNNTAO	=	NEUROPTERAN
AMROAITN	=	TAMANOIR
IPAMSBHAAEN	=	AMPHISBAENA
NUDMATAA	=	TAMANDUA
ECLIDPE	=	PEDICEL

TREE

TAAP	=	TAPA
RALOPP	=	POPLAR
SATEMM	=	STEMMA
NAMEORNT	=	ORNAMENT
AASANCRD	=	SANDARAC
TSINAR	=	STRAIN
OBRS	=	SORB
BLRIFTE	=	FILBERT
PHCEA	=	PEACH
DLAESDT	=	STADDLE
ODAWLODNSA	=	SANDALWOOD
ANAMYOB	=	AMBOYNA

Puzzle # 85
VALUE OF TIME

ILHWE	=	WHILE
MIEPR	=	PRIME
IECIPFCS	=	SPECIFIC
ITGLHF	=	FLIGHT
ROLL	=	ROLL
NEDEEPNTD	=	DEPENDENT
MNIIM	=	MINIM
NRNOALTEMA	=	ORNAMENTAL
FTNIYNII	=	INFINITY
YTASHR	=	TRASHY
IAZLEIIINT	=	INITIALIZE
NCOIRIDTA	=	INDICATOR

OANNWT   =   WANTON

GLRAAARW   =   WARRAGAL

ARFASI   =   SAFARI

MNTAHI   =   MITHAN

EFLL   =   FELL

ETROCV   =   COVERT

EMALTMR   =   TRAMMEL

PHEES   =   SHEEP

EHISRK   =   SHRIEK

EKLA   =   KALE

VELUTTCIA   =   CULTIVATE

CEIERF   =   FIERCE

Puzzle # 87
VIOLIN LESSONS

TAEK	=	TAKE
BUEDSISA	=	DISABUSE
ODNECS	=	SECOND
IARYF	=	FAIRY
OFMRLREY	=	FORMERLY
TOROVSIU	=	VIRTUOSO
EGRB	=	BERG
SLSLUYBA	=	SYLLABUS
DPTERUNAA	=	PANDURATE
ARSPEC	=	SCRAPE
IEACTLR	=	RECITAL
COSANSNEDI	=	DISSONANCE

OCIETNRSDC	=	DISCONCERT
GUTCINT	=	CUTTING
ETCBSKAGA	=	BACKSTAGE
NELGAW	=	WANGLE
RMAWS	=	SWARM
ASET	=	SEAT
NEILLBGEIG	=	NEGLIGIBLE
EGAT	=	GATE
ONAMSISDI	=	ADMISSION
BOTEGLO	=	BOOTLEG
HCLOAR	=	CHORAL
WALZT	=	WALTZ

Puzzle # 89
ENVIRONMENT POLLUTIO

BOACNIUTR	=	INCUBATOR
CNONTOXI	=	NONTOXIC
ATEWAYG	=	GETAWAY
NTSIITORNA	=	TRANSITION
KNOWNUN	=	UNKNOWN
EGLIOTNAUR	=	REGULATION
EHSICPO	=	HOSPICE
EATOLIGB	=	OBLIGATE
AEYBRSPECC	=	CYBERSPACE
ENGRE	=	GREEN
NERASGTR	=	STRANGER
BRSCEBRU	=	SCRUBBER

RUGBY

CAYHR = CHARY

TNSIHASG = HASTINGS

DSHIEL = SHIELD

RDWESDA = EDWARDS

OLOLATBF = FOOTBALL

PROP = PROP

RUEGRG = RUGGER

SPRIPEMIHRE = PREMIERSHIP

FOAYR = FORAY

OSNENOIRCV = CONVERSION

MEAL = MALE

CALHT = LATCH

SHIRT

NDTRSIWBA	=	WRISTBAND
NKECITE	=	NECKTIE
AONMOR	=	MAROON
ELOTCGAEEDL	=	DECOLLETAGE
APOINERF	=	PINAFORE
LMBEPRAEE	=	PERMEABLE
DLUO	=	LOUD
VERRDOSES	=	OVERDRESS
MTLEICOPEN	=	INCOMPLETE
LGYIPMS	=	GYMSLIP
WPITANTAYS	=	PANTYWAIST
DLBIAGIAR	=	GARIBALDI

Puzzle # 92
MONDAY

ADEAH = AHEAD

ELDEUSCH = SCHEDULE

YADWRKO = WORKDAY

DSOHRVEETI = SHROVETIDE

RAEFI = FERIA

KWWROEKE = WORKWEEK

TAUEYSD = TUESDAY

SRCHETT = STRETCH

OCSEL = CLOSE

TRIW = WRIT

RTFEOLVSE = LEFTOVERS

OTORRP = TORPOR

Puzzle # 93

DIVING

KUCD	=	DUCK
DIERPP	=	DIPPER
CESYPAAHTHB	=	BATHYSCAPHE
USPM	=	SUMP
HGYCTOIOLHY	=	ICHTHYOLOGY
PUASC	=	SCAUP
CIBAKHDC	=	DABCHICK
MUJP	=	JUMP
HHEPYTERASB	=	BATHYSPHERE
GNAENT	=	GANNET
LNFOCA	=	FALCON
PERLET	=	PETREL

DANCING

NVIALARC = CARNIVAL

ALED = LEAD

HMOS = MOSH

RAVE = RAVE

ATSXFRIN = TRANSFIX

SEEIPRXET = EXPERTISE

RIQUDLEAL = QUADRILLE

ABAMS = SAMBA

RPTI = TRIP

ERANMG = GERMAN

SLASA = SALSA

EEUROPTTI = PIROUETTE

Puzzle # 95

WORLD

RNCNUIEANT	=	RENUNCIANT
AORNGNE	=	ARGONNE
IWDODLEWR	=	WORLDWIDE
VIWE	=	VIEW
CELPA	=	PLACE
SELME	=	MELES
EIRSA	=	RAISE
ERISPHBEO	=	BIOSPHERE
ONLIITATRSE	=	ORIENTALIST
AKRCC	=	CRACK
SWET	=	WEST
PLNNEOMEAH	=	PHENOMENAL

Puzzle # 96
ONLINE SHOPPING

CIIZTEN = CITIZEN

PCOUNO = COUPON

NAOHRC = ANCHOR

ETKBAS = BASKET

FEDE = FEED

TPLA = PLAT

TPOS = POST

LANHED = HANDLE

OYVENRTNI = INVENTORY

LMLA = MALL

ZGAER = GRAZE

NRORTCBUIOT = CONTRIBUTOR

PHOTO EDITING

RDOOREFPA	=	PROOFREAD
TDOMENEANI	=	EMENDATION
IDTE	=	EDIT
ARIBB	=	RABBI
IBANYEVTLI	=	INEVITABLY
TEFYININS	=	INTENSIFY
GRNIMTMI	=	TRIMMING
APACBKY	=	PAYBACK
EPNO	=	OPEN
CATCH	=	CATCH
SRPAH	=	SHARP
UONFDRGEOR	=	FOREGROUND

Puzzle # 98
HEALTHY SNACKS

COENGONE = ONCOGENE

VGIRUO = VIGOUR

TREYUBT = BUTTERY

ORATWHRME = EARTHWORM

LIHA = HAIL

ISEASRDHN = HARDINESS

IDRECIOP = PERIODIC

AEUNMR = MANURE

TLAOL = ALLOT

RUNPE = PRUNE

CSIESIMTO = SEMIOTICS

EMEIRG = REGIME

Puzzle # 99
RAINBOW

ERLSSUL	=	RUSSELL
GYDUA	=	GAUDY
INOPAEL	=	OPALINE
DAGSAR	=	ASGARD
YIPT	=	PITY
UPPGY	=	GUPPY
OVNIIITECVS	=	VIVISECTION
GUODNS	=	SUNDOG
TDEEIRNICS	=	IRIDESCENT
USCTPREM	=	SPECTRUM
MLDLEAHI	=	HEIMDALL
TAAPRGNEY	=	PAGEANTRY

Puzzle # 100
SWIMMING

HREO	=	HERO
SERESNA	=	ANSERES
VOTIRGE	=	VERTIGO
IKIBIN	=	BIKINI
LMEVU	=	VELUM
OPLHSAEYR	=	HORSEPLAY
MWEMRTSIE	=	SWIMMERET
OSEGO	=	GOOSE
RTPNIAEDUO	=	PORTUNIDAE
OCTIMSHXEA	=	CHEMOTAXIS
LSPA	=	SALP
GINW	=	WING

www.ingramcontent.com/pod-product-compliance
Lightning Source LLC
Chambersburg PA
CBHW081303250726
48662CB00008B/2377